MY
WORD IS MY BOND

MY
WORD IS MY BOND

A Memoir

Paul Weinberg

iUniverse, Inc.
New York Bloomington Shanghai

MY WORD IS MY BOND
A Memoir

iUniverse books may be ordered through booksellers or by contacting:

iUniverse
1663 Liberty Drive
Bloomington, IN 47403
www.iuniverse.com
1-800-Authors (1-800-288-4677)

ISBN: 978-0-595-44625-4 (pbk)
ISBN: 978-0-595-69579-9 (cloth)
ISBN: 978-0-595-88950-1 (ebk)

Printed in the United States of America

THIS BOOK IS DEDICATED to my children, Stacy and Elyce, who at a very young age, lost their ever-loving Grandma Dottie and never had a chance to grow to know her and benefit from her wonderful life experiences. She died in 1976 at the early age of sixty-eight. I was forty years old, Stacy was fourteen, and Elyce was thirteen.

I also dedicate the book to my loving grandchildren, Darci, Molly, Jacob and Nolan, who will learn from it not only the history of their ancestry, but also the loving, thought provoking concepts developed by their ancestors—concepts that have now been passed down from generation to generation.

The author hopes that his grandchildren and all the generations thereafter will benefit from what I've recorded here—actual events, true stories, dialogue—all of which took place many years before they were born, and that they will find in them lessons that will live forever.

Contents

Acknowledgments

IN ORDER FOR THIS BOOK to be brought to life, I had to authenticate actual occurrences within the past one hundred years and more.

The children of Samson Schussler—particularly Mildred Kalikow, Dorothy's younger sister—spent many hours with me discussing the history of that side of the family.

The children of Joseph Schussler, particularly Seymour Schussler, provided firsthand knowledge of life in Austria (part of which is now the Ukraine) at the turn of the twentieth century. He confirmed all that my parents had told me of his introducing them to each other.

Moishe Weinberg's grandson, Saul Sharison, provided information passed on to him by his ancestors about life in the Pale of Settlement. Without his help, I would never have been able to find Moishe Weinberg's descendants.

David Brawerman's youngest child—Lillie Kates, the granddaughter of Meyer and Rizel Brawerman—supplied information handed down through the generations about the arranged marriages and lives of some of her siblings and aunts, starting at the beginning of the twentieth century. She also provided me with the names of Brawerman descendants that helped my research.

George and Irene Burch, my parents' best friends, supplied a wealth of information about my parents' other friends and their relationships, as well as about my father's hardships in his workplace. They only confirmed what my father had told the family every night at the dinner table. The anti-Semitism was a horrible daily experience that may have been the cause of his long illness.

My thanks go to these families for their time, energy, advice, and support—all of which was an enormous help in creating this book.

I thank my brother, Martin, for his impetus in getting me to write about Mom and Dad.

Robert Ludemann of the Merrick Public Library always found the time to help me with historical research. If there was anything that Bob did not know, he had an uncanny knack for locating it very quickly.

Rabbi Maurice Simckes of Temple Israel of South Merrick was the source of much of the Jewish history and found the time to proofread material about Jewish holidays.

Much appreciation to Bobbie Rivere and Judy Shevrin for being so generous with their time in proofreading the manuscript and offering constructive criticism.

For line editing my book, I thank Charles Durham who not only corrected misplaced modifiers but insured proper grammar and consistency.

Any list brings with it a danger of forgetting someone, but I must take that risk so that the following people can be remembered: Myrna Barg, Jeanne Berliner, Pauline Block, Sylvia (Schussler) Brown, Dick Cohen, Elaine and Sandy Cohen, Jack J. Fischer, Estelle Garcia, Gilat (Gur-Arie) Greenberg, Gladys (Weinberg) Goldblatt, Rabbi Scott Hoffman, Ann (Gur-Arie) Kelman, Arthur Kligler, Milton Kligler, Ron (Schussler) Kolman, Barbara and Milton Nash, Elyce (Weinberg) Neuhauser, Mona (Weinberg) Miller, Stacy (Weinberg) Miller, Mabel Moskowitz, Lora and Irwin Neveleff, Francis (Weinberg) Peterson, Jerome Pickholz, Barbara (Kalikow) Regen, Matt Regen, Lillie Reines, Rhoda (Pickholz) Reisner, Karen Sachs, Etta (Schussler) Salant, Sheryl (Weinberg) Scheer, Annette Schussler, Artie and Sheila Schussler, Charles Schussler, Charlie Schussler, Adrienne (Salant) Sills, Maxine Sorokin, Herman Stein, Dr. and Mrs. Eli Stern, Elaine (Schwartz) Weinberg, Edie (Less) Weinberg, Thelma (Geller) Weinberg, and John Westney.

My only disappointment and regret is that I failed to find any ancestors of Samson Schussler's wife, Perl. This was not due to lack of effort on my part. After all research failed, even at the Salt Lake City office of the Church of the Latter Day Saints where several very nice people attempted to locate Perl and her relatives, I found a Russian-speaking rabbi in the Ukraine, with whom I corresponded. The enjoyable part of that correspondence was finding someone who could translate my English letters into Russian and have his correspondence translated back to English. Some of the documents were in Polish and translation to English was another joyride. But not finding any of Perl's ancestors was very disheartening.

I thank my parents, posthumously, for raising me into the person I am.

And finally, I thank my wife who has endured the seven years of my research and writing during which our days were turned into nights and nights were turned into days. Our home office was overloaded with research papers and tapes. Both our desks were consumed with documents. Linda has been very patient with my mood changes as they went up with each research success and down with each research failure. Fortunately, there were more successes than failures, more on the positive side than on the negative.

As a librarian in the Adelphi University Library, Linda was amazed at my abilities to catalog hundreds of interviews and documents, and gave me continuing support that helped build my inner confidence. For that I am very grateful.

Foreword

by Arthur Kurzweil

SINCE EACH OF US HAS two parents, four grandparents, and eight great grandparents, a simple calculation allows us to see that looking at ten generations of a family, each of us has 2,046 ancestors on our family tree. In other words, without even considering uncles, aunts, and cousins, a mere ten generations of direct ancestors adds up to a surprising number of people.

Sometimes I think about those ancestors, and I try to imagine them. What did they look like? What occupied their time? What did they believe in? What were their dreams? Once, I found my mind wandering, and I tried to imagine one of my great-great-great-great grandmothers—whoever she was, wherever she lived, whatever her name. And then I realized that if that one ancestor, *one* out of 2,046 ancestors—in *only* ten generations—had not grown up to have her own children, I simply wouldn't exist.

The lives of our ancestors, their decisions and their fate, have impact on us all. Each of us is a link in a chain.

The act of remembering and recalling a family's history is an ancient and holy one for the Jewish people. Our most ancient ritual, the Passover Seder, is really a simple coming together of the family in order to tell its story. Jews have been doing this for hundreds of generations without fail.

Paul Weinberg continues this sacred tradition as he shares the history you will encounter in these pages. His effort to link us with the past is not simply a gathering of facts or tales. It is, more importantly, a holy act, sacred for its ultimate impact: by reading this family history we actually find ourselves, and we understand how we are really part of one human family. As the Talmud teaches, "Why did God form just one man, Adam, when the world was created? So that nobody can say, 'my ancestor was better than your ancestor.'"

Paul Weinberg has not just written a book. He has fashioned a priceless heirloom whose value, due to the spiritual ideas imbedded in his text, cannot be measured. Human ideals of great proportion, and eternal ideas, dreams, and values can be found here. Their value is immeasurable.

Author's Note

I WROTE THIS BOOK with every effort to make it read as a novel, for in my opinion, a book should excite interest in *everyone* who reads it. As a memoir of my parents, it shows the importance of their background and roots in the development of their social, economic, and religious character.

It was my intense interest in the background of my parents' ancestors that directed this venture into the everyday lives of their parents and grandparents. As you will read, the life of the Jew in Europe was unpleasant. Not only unpleasant, it was downright dangerous. The Jews were considered the quintessential villains, enemies whose lives hampered and even endangered the lives of the non-Jewish populace.

This generational memoir shows how they were persecuted and how they uprooted themselves and their families and ran to another part of the world to escape the persecution.

I found it interesting, even profound, that white European hatred for Jews in the eighteenth and nineteenth centuries carried over into the American white society of the mid-twentieth century—even into the major financial institution in which my father worked.

Prologue

IT WAS COLD AND THE SNOWFLAKES were falling on this particular night in December of 1946. Dad was drawing floor plans on tracing paper on his plan table. The table, with its own fluorescent light and two file cabinets, was perfectly nestled into an alcove in the living room. When Dad was not sitting on his high chair working, the table was neatly adorned with a vinyl cover that my mother had hemmed. The table had a small drawer, handmade by my father, in which he kept a variety of drafting pencils of differing hardness, erasers, erasing shields, and fine sandpaper for sharpening the pencils.

It was a typical scene every night.

Dad would come home from work at about 5:30 and the family would sit down for dinner. Mom made a balanced meal every weekday night. Sometimes it was meat and potatoes with a vegetable or perhaps fish with vegetables. We always started with a big salad. Bread was a staple that we had to eat with the salad.

The Friday night dinner began with Mom lighting the *Shabbos* candles. She would take a shawl, put it over her head, light the three candles, cup her hands around them, and say the prayer that started the Sabbath. After she said, "Good Shabbos," and kissed each one of her men, we sat down to our festive dinner, usually boiled beef that we called flanken. Dad did not eat chicken. He had once seen how chickens were slaughtered, and that sight had forever affected his taste buds.

After dinner, Dad would take a twenty-minute nap while Mom cleaned the kitchen and Marty and I did our homework. He would still be working on his drawings long after his two sons had put their studies away, washed, and gone to bed, always getting a hug and kiss from Mom and a handshake from Dad.

The desire to delay bedtime and the curiosity that a ten-year-old boy possessed that December night brought me to ask Dad many questions. He said he was drawing floor plans for the renovation of a three-story building with a basement, located in lower Manhattan.

"And what do those numbers represent?"

"That is an equation that is used to determine the size of beams used to hold up each floor of the building."

"Where did you find the equations?"

"In a code book."

"What is a code book?"

"It is a description of things required by the city in order to make the buildings safe." He held up a very used black book and said, "These are the laws that I must follow."

"Why are you doing this?" continued the boy.

Somewhat impatiently, my dad told me that the two owners had decided to change the inside of the building so they could rent the apartments. Floundering for more questions, I asked who the two men were. "They are very wealthy homosexuals. Now go to sleep."

My curiosity was piqued. "Is this the first time you've worked on this building?"

His patience was wearing thin when he replied that this was the second time he had worked on the layouts. His two clients had not liked the first plans and asked for revisions. Trying to please my father I said, "Oh, good, that means you'll be making more money."

No, even though the clients had changed their minds about the original sketches, he said that he had given a price on the job and he could not add to it.

"But if they had changed their minds, why can't you change your price?"

As he took my hand and led me into the bedroom, he said something I'll never forget. "My word is my bond."

"What does that mean, Dad?"

Tucking me into bed and turning off the light, he said, "People can steal your money, and people can take your possessions, and people can take all you own. There is one thing that no one can take from you; that is your good word. When you make a promise, never break it. *Your* word is *your* bond. MY WORD IS MY BOND."

Dave at plan table (1944)

Dottie at stove (1944)

1

Push to New York: Dorothy's Family

IT STARTED ON A DIRT ROAD in the small town of Kalush at the foothills of the Carpathian Mountains in the region of Galizia, a province of Stanislaw in the Austro-Hungarian Empire, which is now the Ukraine. Clear water flowed off the mountains and into the Lommica River that ran through the outskirts of the town. Kalush was about four hundred miles southwest of Kiev and 260 miles south east of Warsaw, the capital of Poland.[1] Life was not good in that area, especially for Jews. Children were put to work at young ages to help the family survive, and many did not go to school. For Jews across Eastern Europe, poverty and prejudice were part of everyday life. They were not allowed to own their own land and could only work in certain professions. Without special governmental authorization, they were not permitted to attend universities, even if they had made it out of elementary school.

Batzalal Schussler struggled to make a living. He was a very religious man, a *Rosh Yeshiva*, a rabbinic instructor also called the headmaster.[2] In those days, Yeshiva was for boys only, and it took some from high school right through college. His wife, the former Schprintza Herzfeld, and their seven children lived in a dormitory-style house where everyone slept in the same room. While the kids slept, more kids were made. The toilet was in a separate outside enclosure called an outhouse. Taking a bath was a luxury reserved for a different person every night. Sometimes, two or three children took a bath on the same night, in the same tub, at the same time. There was no running water; water was provided by an outdoor pump. The tub was inside the house, and for baths, they boiled water in pots on the stove. If the supply of water was scarce, the girls went to a public bath for women only.

The side of the street on which they lived had only one other residence. The other side had a slaughterhouse and a butcher shop. There was always a smell of beef in the air—dead beef. Behind their house was a Catholic church. Playtime for the poor Jewish boys was limited because they were always studying. Their recreation consisted of running around and playing tag or playing wheel. That competition had each boy hitting a hanging wheel with a stick to see who could make the wheel spin the longest. They dared not dirty or rip their clothing; it had to last the week.

For several reasons, the Jewish people lived near each other in what were called ghettos. The first reason was that the non-Jewish community did not, in general, like the Jews and did not want to live with or near them. The second reason was that the Jews found comfort among themselves. They had different customs, different languages and, most importantly, different houses of worship. Yetta and Usher Kimmel lived very close to Batzalal and Schprintza. Yetta was the sister of Batzalal, and, when the two siblings got married, they found living near each other very pleasant.

Batzalal and Schprintza had seven children: Shmiel (1877), Shimshon (1879), Lietcha (1881), Jacob (1883), Joseph (1886), Max (1891), and Oscar (1896).

Usher and Yetta had one daughter, Perl (1883), who called her uncle Batzalal, "Feter" (uncle) and her aunt Schprintza, "Tanta" (aunt).

Shimshon Aron Schussler, who was born in 1879, was four years older than his first cousin Perl, but the close proximity of the families brought the two into frequent contact. Although they were cousins, they felt an attraction to each other—like opposite poles of magnets. As they grew up, their shared fondness blossomed and they found they enjoyed being together. Sometimes they would meet near the sandy beach and run through the woods. After exhaustion caught up with them, they would lie on the aromatic country grass, enjoy the sweet air, and talk about the future.

Shimshon was a handsome man—not tall by today's standards; he stood at five feet four inches, being about two inches shorter than Perl. He, like Perl, had brown hair that matched the color of his eyes. She was a strong woman in stature and had a kindly nature. Although she was taller than Shimshon, they made a nice looking couple, and they were in love.

But things were not good in Austria-Hungary before the turn of the century. The economy was on a downslide, and people, especially the Jews, were afraid of the Kaiser. Shimshon's parents told him about the horrible massacres—called pogroms—of the Jewish people, that were taking place in Eastern Europe. Jewish houses of worship were so scorned, it was difficult to pray as one pleased, and so they secretly used individual homes as synagogues.

Shimshon and Perl decided to wait until the economy improved before marrying and raising a family. But things did not get better. In fact, things in Europe were on the steady decline. Shimshon knew he couldn't raise a family without having a job that would support them. He worked as the head dressmaker from dawn to dusk, five and a half days a week for a small company in Kalush, but would come home with so little money that it would never support two, and even less, a family. He had little free time and no luxuries. Was there any reason to believe life would improve?

He discussed the situation with his older brother Schmiel. His other brothers and his sister were too young to understand the problems facing a man in love. His parents, Schprintza and Batzalal, had trouble of their own and couldn't be bothered by the impetuous ideas of their son Shimshon. But Shimshon was very smart. He did not have an education like the rich people, but he was intuitive. He heard about the American laws restricting immigration passed these last twenty-five years. And there were soon to be new laws that would fix quotas and ban certain groups of people from entering the United States. He could not wait any longer.

He spoke to his cousin and good friend Itcha Steg who was seven years his senior and the owner of a very successful clothing business in Kalush. Itcha was always challenging Shimshon with mathematical problems, some of which were related to his business, and Shimshon always quickly solved them. Itcha had already immigrated to the United States, set up residence in New York City, and begun to successfully manufacture and sell clothing. He lived near the Schusslers and had returned for his wife, Ruchal. Shimshon pleaded with his recalcitrant cousin to take him with them. But his cousin did not want to offend the Schussler family, so he went to Schprintza and Batzalal and offered to sponsor their son if they would allow him to emigrate. They agreed. Shimshon was going to America to live out his dream, where he could marry and earn a decent living so he could raise a family without fear of anyone going hungry.

It may sound like an easy decision to emigrate. But think about the traumatic task this young man was taking on. He woke up one morning to say good-bye to everyone and everything he had ever known and would probably never see again. Good-bye to his mother and father. Good-bye to his brothers and sister. Good-bye to all his friends. Good-bye to his neighbors and neighborhood, the food, the culture, the language—and to his sweetheart. All this was after months of applications, permits, passports, and visas. It was not a happy day for Shimshon, but he was hoping it was the first day of the rest of a better life.

On November 7, 1902, he boarded the railroad with provisions given him by his mother and a Bible given to him by his father. Since there was no direct rail link between Kalush and Bremen, he had to first travel to Warsaw, wait a day for the next train to Berlin, and from there, it was another train to the port city—not what one would call a relaxing trip. As a matter of fact, it was a storybook adventure of eluding the Kaiser's police. Shimshon was of conscription age. The polizi were going through the trains leaving Warsaw, taking the young boys off and putting them into the army. Shimshon found himself running from car to car in an effort to avoid arrest. Sometimes, when the train slowed, he would hop off the front and hop back on at the end of the train to avoid the polizi. He finally arrived in Bremen, Germany, a busy city he had never seen before. But he was not yet free. He had to fill out forms for boarding the ship. The form listed the age of the passengers, and he wrote that he was twenty-one years old. He made his way to the harbor and stood in endless lines with thousands of other people.

Talk about confusion, excitement and fear! Talk about the cost of the ticket that would carry him to the New World! The ticket had cost his mother and father 150 deutschemarks, which at that time was the cost of a month's food for the family. After days of waiting, along with about two thousand other passengers, he finally boarded the ship called the *Main*, and went to the lowest deck—steerage—where he would sleep in a communal room with several hundred people and no windows, using his small valise as a pillow. Finally, on November 15, 1902, the ship set sail for New York.

It was the early morning two weeks later when he heard a distinct and sudden change in the sound of the engine. The early risers up on deck caught sight of a gray strip of land someone had called "the long island." There were cries of joy in many languages, but the one word that was the same in all languages was "America." Many of those peering at the coast broke into tears. And so, on December 1, 1902, Shimshon Aron, at the age of twenty-three, landed on Ellis Island, and registered as Samson Aaron Schussler.

Like all the other immigrants, as he paused, a doctor looked hard at his face, eyes, hair, neck and hands, all the while asking questions about his age and work to test for alertness. Then he passed into another room, and there was examined for a plethora of diseases specifically mentioned by law as reasons for deportation—diseases such as tuberculosis, leprosy, and contagious skin disease. The last room was for the dreaded "eye men" who were looking for symptoms of a blinding disease called *trachoma*. Immigrants who had it were sure to be sent back to Europe. After Samson passed all these tests, an inspector asked a myriad of questions to establish what he did, if there was a job waiting for him, where he would live, and how much money he had. After about five hours on Ellis Island, he received a curt nod from the inspector, walked down a dark corridor and through doors marked "Push To New York," bought a ferry ticket, and finally landed in lower Manhattan. There, his smiling and happy cousins, Itcha and Ruchal Steg met him and took him home to live with them. After finding a job as a dressmaker trainee earning three dollars a week, he was ready to get his own apartment.

At the turn of the century, one of the most crowded neighborhoods where immigrant Jews settled was the Lower East Side of New York City. The Jewish people started to move north into the single digit street numbers to avoid the overcrowding and yet still be near people who spoke their language, enjoyed the same music and comedy, read the same books, and of course, practiced the same religion.

Living with landsmen (countrymen) made it easier to socialize and to feel a part of the community and yet begin to assimilate with native-born Americans. For some, there was a feeling that they were strangers in America, and a part of them always remained in the Old World. For others, the neighborhood made it easy to shop for familiar foods, and was a place where they could buy a Jewish newspaper and pray without persecution.

In New York, the immigrant clothing industry workers were packed into small, crowded rooms every day for ten hours or more. The conditions were so bad they called them sweatshops. The work and poverty were hard to endure, but were nothing new for many of those who knew what it felt like to go hungry. The hazardous conditions under which they worked attracted national attention in March of 1911, when a disastrous fire swept through the Triangle Waist Company killing about 150 people.

Despite the adverse conditions, Samson's boss soon found that his employee was an excellent craftsman and promoted him with a slight raise (at that time considered a *substantial* raise). Since Samson needed more money to be able to bring the family to America, he became a jobber. He would take home material and, in his own small apartment, work longer hours to cut and sew and complete dresses, sometimes called "shirtwaists," and sell the completed items to his boss. He solicited other people to work for him in order to make a profit on the labor of others. At last, with the entrepreneurial knowledge he had gained in Europe, he was able to save enough money to bring his sweetheart and siblings from the Old Country. He rented a small apartment and wrote Perl and his brothers that they should come to America. But his older brother, Schmiel, and his young sister, Leitcha, wanted to remain in Europe.

In 1903, earning close to seven dollars a week plus his jobber income, Samson had enough money to send for Perl and his brother Joseph, and on different dates, they set out from Kalush to come to the shores of the United States. Joseph arrived in 1903. Perl arrived in New York harbor on October 27, 1904.[3] Joseph worked for Samson for two years but did not like the life in New York and returned to Europe where he would remain for another sixteen years before returning to America with his wife and two sons.

It was both a happy and a melancholy day when Samson, without any of his family present, married Perl—or Pepi, which was the name she preferred—on November 11, 1905.[4] After a simple, small wedding ceremony in front of Rabbi Issac Edelman, they went to live in their new three-room apartment at 223 East Seventh Street in Manhattan.

Mary, their first child, was born on July 30, 1906, followed by Dora on July 1, 1908.[5] Things were going well, but tragedy was about to strike.

2

The Pale of Settlement and
Lodz: David's Family

PRIOR TO THE FIRST PARTITION OF POLAND in 1772, the Russian government made explicit attempts to ban Jews from Russia. Then Poland was carved up by Russia, Prussia, and Austria and into Russian hands came the two areas we know today as Poland and the Ukraine. Almost overnight, hundreds of thousands of Jews were added to the Russian Empire. How contradictory were the Russians; on one hand, they tried to deny Jews the right to live in their country, and on the other, they annexed land that added so many more Jews to their population.

By the laws of 1795 and 1835, the Russian government limited its new Jews to the newly annexed areas, later known as the Pale of Settlement, which ran from the Black Sea on the southwestern end to the Baltic Sea on the northwestern end.[6] The Pale was divided into nineteen provinces called guberniyas, and each guberniya had several small towns or villages called *shtetls*.[7] In 1882, more than 1.5 million Russian Jews who had managed to live outside the Pale were forced into it, so that by 1885, there were 4 million Jews living in the Pale. Four percent of the territory of the Russian Empire held 94 percent of the Jewish population.[8]

A turning point in the history of the Russian Jews came in 1881. They were unable to persuade the Russian hierarchy that Jews merited a share in its future, and their hopes were badly shaken, perhaps destroyed.[9] In March of 1881, revolutionaries assassinated Alexander II. The regime was compelled to protect itself, and the Russian government used the Jews as the scapegoat. The notion was that they were responsible for the misfortunes of the nation. Anti-Jewish riots broke out in a number of towns in southern Russia.[10]

Moishe Weinberg, with his wife Ruchal and two daughters, Jennie and Shandle, were living in a shtetl and managing rather well. They lived at the flour mill that he owned in a southern border town. During the warm weather, the peasant farmers would bring their different grains to the mill to be ground into flour and then sold. His mill, the only one in the small town, was very busy during the warm season when the crops were being harvested. He invested his handsome profits in real estate and eventually owned extensive property within the community.

Moishe was a tall man, thin all his life. When he wasn't working at the mill, he would walk tall, wearing a black frock coat, white hair combed straight back and a long snow-white beard, which made him look like an orthodox man. He had blue, pearly grey eyes and rarely smiled. When he collected his rents, he moved with a cocky stride, knowing he could evict anyone who did not pay.

Although Moishe's oldest daughter, Jennie, was an extremely bright young lady who absorbed his business acumen, it was not considered proper to prime a female for business. A girl was to marry, bear children, and be subservient to her husband who would make all family and business decisions. The birth of another daughter, Shandle, in 1883, did not please Moishe. He wanted a son who had good business sense, who would help him at the mill and, eventually, take over the family enterprise. Finally, in 1884, Ruchal presented him with a son they named Nusan. Moishe was thrilled with his son. The earth revolved around the boy. Everything was as perfect as could be. When Nusan was four years old, like all the other Jewish boys of his age, he started to receive a Jewish education.

However, Alexander III, Czar until 1894, in 1882 had passed "Temporary Laws" predicated on a governmental commission's report that said Jewish exploitation had caused the pogroms. In an attempt to halt the flood of Jews now seeking entry to secondary schools and universities, the number of Jewish students in those schools was limited by law to 10 percent.[11] Nusan was not in the 10 percent category, and went to religious school until he was ten years old. His father felt it was more important to get an education at the mill than a formal education in school. That decision would negatively affect the rest of Nusan's life. Until he left school, he would report to the mill to do miscellaneous chores for his father every afternoon. He had good hands, was very powerful, and learned quickly, so by the time he was ten, he was not only able to complete the tasks of any of the workers, but he completed them faster and better. Moishe was the role model for his son, who emulated him. Moishe was the king of his family, and Nusan was going to be the next king.

In 1894, Nicholas II became Russia's last Czar.[12] He observed Japan's victory over the Chinese in the Sino-Japanese War of 1894-95 after which Japan took possession of Port Arthur on the Manchurian Peninsula.[13] The Czar wanted to keep his power by keeping the Russian people busy. So he concluded an alliance with China against Japan and in the process won rights to extend the Trans-Siberian Railroad across Chinese held Manchuria to the Russian Seaport of Vladivostok, thus gaining control of an important strip through Manchurian territory.[14]

Meanwhile, on April 15, 1896, Ruchal gave birth to their fourth child, a girl whom they named Fannie.[15] Although a series of bad harvests were causing starvation among the peasants, Moishe survived. He had hedged his income between the mill and real estate investments so that financially, things were good. The revolutionary movement had been kept in check; as a Jew he couldn't have asked for anything more than what he had.

It was about this time that the Japanese were concerned about the spread of Russian influence in Manchuria and Korea and tried, unsuccessfully, to work out a treaty with Russia.[16] As a result, Japan started to build up troops in preparation for a war against Russia. The Czar was not blind to this build up, and, although he had no fear of the small Japanese army, he decided to increase Russian forces as well.[17]

Moishe corresponded with his friend, Meyer Brawerman, who lived on Piotrkowska Street, the Jewish Street in Lodz, and compared the life of the Jewish people in the two cities. As a businessman, Moishe was always thinking ahead. What would he do if the powerful Russian Empire came crashing down on the Jewish people? What if the Czar conscripted the Jews into his army to fight the Japanese? Where would he go? What would he do? Nusan was a teenager, and the Czar just might want him to fight for the Russian cause. Moishe always wanted to be with "his people, his clan." The future seemed bleak in Russia. There seemed no choice, and he started divesting himself of some properties.

The Temporary Laws and other policies had been continued under the new Czar. And the Czar made things even worse by giving free rein to the anti-Semitic press. But Moishe and several other Jews worked even harder to achieve what they conceived of as a happy and successful life.

The Czar was not happy that even *some* Jews were doing well during those hard times, and he now wanted them out of the shtetl. In many communities, half the Jewish population depended on charity to survive.[18] Not only were they ordered to move, they were not even allowed to sell their properties. It was all just as well. The pogroms were getting worse. Moishe had to get out of Russia while he had a chance. Very surreptitiously, he sold more of his properties at a fraction of their value and left Russia with what little money he had salvaged. He took his family and headed west where things were not very much better.

Lodz [19]

LODZ, A SMALL VILLAGE chartered in 1423, became a haven for Jews in the first half of the nineteenth century, and within a relatively short period of time grew into the second largest city in Poland, after Warsaw, the capital. The Jewish community grew as fast as the city itself. The Jewish population represented a strong minority in several other big cities in Poland such as Krakow, Poznan, and Wilno, but nowhere did they exert such a strong influence as in Lodz, which came to be nicknamed, the "Jewish City of Lodz." So many Jews came there to live that it appeared they would eventually match the number of non-Jews. This was unprecedented.

Lodz was not like other Polish cities. It was the youngest city, without history and without tradition. Its history and culture were in the making, and the Jews, due to their initiative, energy, industry and intelligence, were taking an active part in it. The Polish middle class occupied mainly governmental and communal offices, leaving the field open for Jews to become professionals; lawyers, medical practitioners, engineers, etc. Although there was anti-Semitism from the time the city was first settled by the Germans, and though the loyalties of the population swung from the left to right and back again, the Jews felt very comfortable among themselves because of their numbers. They controlled two of the three Polish daily papers, so the press was never negative toward them. Even the Germans collaborated with them at election time. The cooperation between the minorities was the best form of defense against Polish nationalism.

This was a good place for Moishe and Ruchal to bring their children. The schools were not restricted. As a matter of fact, some of the best high schools in Poland were the First and the Second Jewish High School for Boys and the Jewish High School for Girls. These were founded and maintained by the Jewish Society for High Schools in Poland.

Moishe had been writing to several of his friends and felt that this growing Jewish town would be the best haven for his family. It would be a fine atmosphere in which to raise their youngest child, Fannie. Yes, he would move to Piotrkowska Street and be close to the Brawerman Family.

The Brawermans were a humble family, living in humble surroundings. There were six people now in the Brawerman house. It was 1899, and two of the six children, Miriam, born in 1876, and her sister Vittel, born in 1877, were already married and living close by. David was engaged to a woman by the name of Rotza, and they were planning a turn of the century wedding. Meyer, David's father, and Rotza's father arranged the match.[20] It was an accommodation on

Meyer's part. Rotza's father had promised a handsome dowry, and there was great disappointment when he broke that promise.

Rizel and Meyer Brawerman were proud of their children and happy that the two oldest girls were married and having families of their own. Hinde, the third daughter, born in 1880, was closing in on her twentieth birthday, and Meyer was worried. He was a religious man, and, according to the Bible, if a father does not find a husband for his daughter while she is young, she may become unchaste, and he will have transgressed.[21] He certainly did not want that on his conscience.

Meyer had been corresponding with his friend Moishe who lived in the Pale and said that the pogroms were getting worse and he was leaving with his wife, three daughters and his son. Moishe said his son was finished with school and had been working with him.

Oh, thought Meyer, what a nice opportunity for both families. It would be so nice if Moishe and he could make a *shitach*, a match, between his daughter and Moishe's son. Parents usually arranged marriages at that time, and it was usual to marry within the clan.[22] Little did he know that Moishe's son, Nusan, was now only fifteen years old.

By the turn of the century, Shoel, who was born in 1882, was a young man, working to earn enough to support a family of his own as soon as he found himself a good woman. His two sisters were married and already raising families, and his twenty-one-year-old brother was engaged. It was his turn now to marry and leave the home. Once his older sister Hinde married, his fourteen-year-old brother Sam, would be the only child who would remain with Mom and Dad.

From a family standpoint, Lodz was a perfect setting for matchmakers. It seemed as if young people were just waiting for the start of the twentieth century so they could marry.

David and Rotza were married in 1901, and Rotza gave birth to Chana on May 15, 1903. Shortly thereafter, they decided to join their friends and family in Canada. There, David became a harness maker, a trade in which he proved successful. He went into a secondary business and sold shoes, and this business was also a success. He was doing so well that he opened a secondhand store and sold antiques.[23]

Hinde, at the age of twenty-one, married Nusan, then seventeen, in 1901 and was soon pregnant. On December 25, 1902, she gave birth to their first child, Isador.

Seventeen-year-old Nusan Weinberg, now with a wife and child but without a formal education to launch him into a profession and unprepared to work in any business other than a flour mill, was bouncing from job to job trying to make enough money to support a family. Then, on September 18, 1904, Hinde gave birth to their second child, Frances.

Frustrated by his failure in business, Nusan decided to head for greener pastures. So, in January of 1905, with his wife, two-year-old son and four-month-old daughter, he set sail for Canada. Upon landing, Nusan and Hinde registered their names as Nathan and Annie, but sadly, even the change of name and environment did not change things for the Weinberg family. Nathan continued to flounder. His wife's brother David tried to help by suggesting the shoe repair business. After all, people had to get their shoes repaired, and David might even be able to send some business his way. By mid-year, Annie was again pregnant and, on March 17, 1906 gave birth to their third child, a son they named David.

MEANWHILE, IN THE TOWN OF KALUSH, Austria-Hungary, there lived a handsome man, Joe Share, the youngest of five brothers, who was not educated like other Jewish young men. So in 1901, he decided to leave Kalush and get a new start in the Jewish City of Lodz. The Russian Army, to thwart the threat of the Japanese, was at that time conscripting one man from every family. After arriving in Lodz, Joe Share decided to marry to avoid going to the war.

He met and married Jennie Weinberg, Moishe's oldest daughter, in 1903. She did what most other Jewish women did at that time; became pregnant. Joe's idea to marry to avoid the draft did not work, and he was forcibly conscripted into the Czarist Army. The very business-minded Jennie, in the meantime, opened a restaurant and, despite having a son, ran it very successfully. She catered to the officers and "high officials" of the Russian Army as well as to the border guards, and she knew them all by first name. They, in turn, brought their men to her restaurant. It was a win/win situation for everyone.

Because of the lack of medical attention and medical knowledge in Europe at the turn of the century, Jennie's child died. She was very bitter and decided that if she were going to have more children with Joe, she had better get Joe out of the country before the Czar sent him to Siberia. She felt that once he was sent to Siberia, he would never return.

So Jennie "arranged," with one of the high officials for her husband to be granted "leave" for a few weeks before being sent to the front lines in Siberia. Once that was arranged, she bribed the friendly border guards to allow him to leave the country, and he ran for his life. Joe, with the money Jennie gave him, hopped on and off trains, hid during the day, and ran at night, just to get to a port that would take him across the ocean to the United States.

He arrived in New York in 1904, changed his name to Sharison, and set up a restaurant. Although the restaurant was not terribly successful, he made enough money to send for Jennie, who joined him one year later, in 1905. Again, she immediately became pregnant and in 1906 gave birth to a son, Saul.

Joe gladly gave the restaurant's management responsibilities to Jennie who turned it into a thriving business. She followed in the footsteps of her father by investing her profits in real estate, soon owned vast properties in Lower Manhattan, and became a very wealthy woman. Jennie wanted the Weinberg family to be together, so she sent for her young brother, Nathan.[24]

Nathan, Annie, Isidor, Francis, and David arrived in the United States in 1908.[25] Jennie put Nathan into the shoe repair business, where he made an adequate living to support a still growing family.

Thirteen years later was a proud time in the life of Nathan Weinberg. On March 10, 1921, seven days before David's fifteenth birthday, Nathan received his Certificate of Naturalization and became a citizen of the United States of America.[26]

As a matter of record, it is worthy of note that David Weinberg was born in Montreal, Canada. This fact is supported not only by many discussions David had with his two sons, one of whom is the author, but by the author's discussions with David's parents, sisters, and brothers, as well as by the 1920 United States Federal Census[27] and his application for a social security account number[28]

However, David wanted the records to show that he had been born in the United States. Armed with a copy of the *1915 State of New York Census*[29] and the *1910 United States Census*,[30] both showing he was born in the United States, on June 6, 1962, David was issued a delayed registration certificate of birth,[31] certifying that he had been born in New York City.

3

Dorothy's Childhood

AND THE GOOD LORD in his infinite wisdom was working on his fifty-year plan, just before the turn of the century.

She will be beautiful, graceful, and have a wonderful disposition. To be sure, she will be a lady with a pretty voice and long fingers to play the keys. Patience and loving will always be her virtues. This girl with a quick smile will embrace the Jewish religion.

So it was written, and so it came to pass on this cloudy, rainy Wednesday, on the first day of July in the year 1908, Dora Schussler was born in the home of her parents, Samson and Perl Schussler, at 223 East Seventh Street in the City of New York. Her eyes were blue and her fingers long. She was pretty. She was perfect in every way.

It was a day when horse-drawn cars were still transferring people across town because there was no electric power, and a New York judge had ordered the discontinuance of free transfers. The *New York Times* was selling for one cent, and Vogel Brothers Men's Shop was advertising suits at $15 and a pair of shoes at $2.50.

She would call her father Papa, her mother Mama, and her older sister Mary—named after *Mima* (aunt) Miriam. Dora was named after a deceased cousin, Davora, and therefore inherited her Hebrew name. She was a very bright baby. But Samson had wanted a son.

Freda was born into the family in 1910, and Dora got another sister, Evelyn in 1912. The fifth girl in the family was Mildred, born on March 18, 1914. Then, four months later, on July 29, 1914, the family's first tragedy hit; four-year-old Freda died of a burst appendix.

Although Papa was doing an excellent job for his boss, the raises he was receiving were small. There was a depression in the United States, and everyone was tightening his belt. There were now four children sleeping in one bedroom, and Mama was again pregnant. So in the fall of the year 1915, Dora found herself moving with her parents and sisters into a larger apartment at 228 East Seventh Street, just across the street, where she would live for the next eleven years. On February 21, 1916, Samson Schussler got his wish—his wife gave him a son. They named him Oscar; after his mother's father, but his Hebrew name was Usher.

Even though there was a war in Europe, things for the Schussler family were good.

Samson, needing more money to support his growing family, subsidized the immigration of his younger brother Max to the United States, and they went into business making girls' blouses. And so was born The Daisy Waist Company, a prospering joint venture.

Max was a fantastic public relations man, and Samson was a fantastic blouse designer and tailor. Together, Samson and Max brought over their youngest brother, also named Oscar, to work as a part-time gofer—an errand boy. Samson sponsored him, and Max paid his passage. Poor Oscar, who came to the United States in 1912 at the age of sixteen, was working to pay back his brothers, so that his take-home pay was virtually nothing.

Tragedy and a deep trauma hit the Schussler family again when Evelyn, at the age of six, died in the worst epidemic ever to hit the United States.[32] The influenza epidemic in 1918 took the lives of about six hundred thousand people. A person might wake up in the morning as healthy as could be and be dead by sundown. The country was running out of caskets. People were afraid to be with other people for fear of contracting the disease. If you had to go outdoors, you wore a mask, which didn't really help. The Daisy Waist Company folded.

As young as she was, with the death of two sisters and her father without a job, ten-year-old Dora had already seen the ultimate in family tragedy. The memory of the death of her young sister to the dreaded influenza would stay with her for the next eighteen years, when her second son would be born.

As 1918 wound down, things started to improve. World War I ended, the epidemic was over, Papa landed a job, and Mama was pregnant again. Samson decided that his two-year-old son, Oscar, needed a brother. On January 10, 1919, just six days before the ratification of the only constitutional amendment that would be repealed—the prohibition amendment[33]—a new member of the family was introduced to the world. Yetta was born.

But Samson wanted another son, and he finally got his wish. On December 17, 1920, another boy joined the family and was named Charles after his father's father, Batzalal. Now there were eight people occupying the one-bedroom apartment. The six children were squeezed into the living room and they loved it. Dora's sister Mildred, said, "It was great. We didn't know any better. If there had been fifteen children in that room, we wouldn't have known any better."[34]

The important thing in those days was to teach the girls *Yiddishkeit* (Jewishness) so they would be prepared to make good wives and good mothers for the next generation. Mary and Dora were very much into the Jewish religion and even helped out the younger brothers and sisters with Hebrew teaching as well as schoolwork.

The typical day began at about seven o'clock in the morning. With only one bathroom in the house, everyone arose at a different time. Papa had to be at work at 8:30, so he was the first one into the bathroom—after Mama. Mama was the first one up because she had to prepare breakfast for the army. Breakfast usually consisted of either cold or hot cereal, and bread and milk. While Papa was finishing breakfast and readying himself for the day, Dora and her sister Mary were getting dressed and washed, readying themselves for school.

After school, the children would play with some of their friends for about two hours. Dora had four girls she was close to in high school. They all lived nearby, and the bond forged in elementary and high school kept some of them together through their married years. Rose Braunstein was Dora's closest friend. Then there was Mabel Pollack, Gussie Saposnick, and Esther Zwering. Dora was also friendly with Itcha and Ruchal Steg's daughter Ann—whose married name was Phillips—and a cousin Ethel Balk.

The neighbors of the Schussler family were Weiss, Reifler, Zering, Gold, Pachtinger, Cohen, Bitterman, Greenberg, Elzenfond, Schlessinger, Pressman, and Pollack. The present whereabouts of those families is not known.

Afternoon playtime ended, and Dora and her sisters would return to the house and help Mama with the house chores. They would clean, dust, sweep, and help in the preparation of dinner. Mama kept them busy. After dinner, it was homework, wash, and off to bed. The lights went out early because Papa went to sleep no later then ten o'clock.

The weekends were somewhat different. One of the girls washed the kitchen and bathroom floors late on Friday afternoon, and Mama would cover the clean floor with newspaper to keep off the dust. When Papa came home, the newspaper was removed, and the floor was damp-cleaned again to remove any newsprint from the linoleum.

The *Shabbos* dinner started with the *Motzee*—a prayer *over* the *chaleh* that Mama had baked, then chicken soup, chicken, and potatoes. The children were not allowed to go outside and play because it was Shabbos. Playing, writing, listening to the radio or playing records, putting the lights on or off were not allowed. Nothing that resembled work was allowed in the Schussler household on Shabbos.

On Saturday morning, the girls would get up first and prepare the breakfast for Papa, Mama, and Oscar, who went to *shul*—synagogue—with them. When the boys reached the age of four, they began going to shul with Papa. Oscar, who was able to read the Torah by the age of seven, was the star of Papa's eye.[35] Then the girls made breakfast for themselves. Dora would spend the day reading and studying. Not that her parents looked on the studying as a good thing; all they wanted was for the girls in the family to get married by the time they were twenty years old.

Sunday was the one day you did what you wanted. Well ... *almost* what you wanted. Dora would call on her friends or they on her, and they would idle the day away. Most of the activities were made up of things that did not cost any money. Sometimes, in their earlier childhood, they would take needle and thread and sew doilies from rags while sitting on the stoop. Or they would make a "horse rein," made by winding leftover wool and thread that Papa brought home around the metal prongs that were inserted into empty thread spools. Hop Scotch, jump rope, and jacks were other games they played.

Dora had no dolls and no carriages. Neither Mary nor Dora ever owned or played with dolls. The family was growing, and the girls had their baby sisters on whom they showered their female tenderness. When Dora got older, she inherited a pair of used roller skates from one of the neighbors. When she outgrew the skates, she passed them down to her younger sister, Mildred, who passed them on to her much younger sisters. There was no such thing as a *club*. You had friends, and you played whenever the free time allowed.

Dora and her siblings did not get into trouble. They were very respectful to their parents. This came from a combination of their upbringing and their fear of their father who would not spare his hand or belt on the part of their body used mostly for sitting. They did not smoke and did not stay out late. Although there wasn't a curfew, they knew that when it started to get dark, they were expected home. When friends visited their house, they too had to leave to get home before it got dark. There was no such thing as a sleepover for friends, because there was no room for friends to sleep over.

Although, at that time, there was no such thing as a *bat mitzvah* for girls, Samson wanted his daughters to have a good Jewish education. He hired a rabbi to come to the house and teach Dora and her sisters about the religion, the language, and the holidays and traditions, so they could carry on the religion for the future generations and be able to teach their children what is meant by *Yom Kippur, Rosh Hashona, Pesach* (Passover), *Purim* and all the other holidays.

Dora was growing into a beautiful young lady, compassionate of others, attentive and smart, well spoken and talented.

It was about this time that Samson's brother, Joseph, returned to the United States with his wife Ruchal and their two sons, Seymour and Charlie, and rented an apartment at 279 East Seventh Street, just one block east of Samson and Pepi. Although Seymour was a few months younger than Dora, they became fast friends and saw each other at least once a week and on weekends. He was a very bright young boy. Every Jewish boy in Europe was educated in Judaism and learned to read and write, not only Hebrew, but also five or six other languages. Although denied entrance to the public schools, they all went to *cheder* (Hebrew elementary school) and had a very strict learning experience. This was also a means of survival. Borders were changing so rapidly in Europe that one had to fluently read, write, and understand all the languages of the surrounding countries. Charlie said, "That is what made the Jews as great as they were and are. They go by the book—*their* Book." They study the Talmud and know the philosophical history of the world.[36]

Dora had a flare for music. She started music lessons when she passed the age of fifteen. Samson loved to dance, and Dora was the one with whom he wanted to dance. If there were such a thing as the family "princess," the title belonged to her. Now called Dorothy by her friends, sometimes shortened to Dottie, this beautiful and graceful young lady who seemed to elude household chores, found that the young men were flocking to her. Eddie Marmel was one of those who couldn't keep away from her, and they both enjoyed each other's company until he went off to the University of Alabama to become a lawyer. After he left, Dottie never saw him again. However, she was very popular and dated a lot during those years.

The Christa Dora House was a music school for the poor children in the neighborhood. It was there that a young teenager could learn how to dance and sing and play an instrument. They would have dances and parties where Dottie and her friends would go to meet other young people and, every so often, get a date. Single dating was frowned on when you first met someone of the opposite sex, so Dottie would usually double date with one of her good friends or with Seymour Schussler.

When Dottie turned eighteen, she took voice lessons, which in those days were called "singing lessons." Her sister, Mildred, took dancing lessons. The same teacher, Professor Gotera, who lived across the street from the Schusslers, taught both.

Samson was very proud of his girls. While one sang, the other one danced. At the young age of five, Charles was enjoying his sisters' singing, and it made a lasting impression on him.

Dottie was very conscious of her appearance. She dressed well, wore a clean white blouse and a blue or brown middy skirt with a gold tie to school, groomed herself, and, although it was not the custom back then to shower every day, she was one who did.

She scrubbed her face several times a day to keep it from being shiny, but every so often, got a black head. In the living room, there stood a highboy phonograph, and on its front cover was an identification tag so polished that the family used it as a mirror. One day Dottie stood in front of the phonograph and squeezed one blackhead on her face in order to remove it. As her sister Mildred secretly watched, Dottie keeled over and fainted.[37] What hurt her more; the knock that she received from the handle of the phonograph or the blow to her ego? No one ever found out.

If a girl was not married by the age of twenty, some began to think she would be an old maid. True to form, Mary met Sol Pickholz, and they planned a wedding for May 26, 1926.

It so happened that Mama and Papa had decided to complete the family after the wedding when the oldest girl moved out. Yes, Mama was in her eighth month at the wedding of her oldest daughter and gave birth on June 30, 1926, to Annette, the last of the Schussler children and the first and only child born with the help of a doctor.

Mary and Sol had their first child one year later. Rhoda was born on November 13, 1927, making one-year-old Annette an aunt at a very early age.

Dottie was now nineteen years old, working for David Davidoff Dress House on Seventh Avenue in Manhattan as a secretary, and had started dating a fellow by the name of Harry Bregman. The relationship intensified, and they became engaged in October of 1928. Things were going as well as would be expected in a fairy tale book. A poor girl meets and marries a rich prince, and they live happily ever after. Besides, she had reached the age when a young woman was *expected* to get married.

Her bother Oscar, who had finished *Talmud Torah* in Manhattan and *Machziki Talmud Torah* in Brooklyn, was being groomed to be a rabbi. It was the practice of the Schussler boys to go from one school to the next to be taught everything about Judaism. Oscar would say that he never had a single moment for himself, that he had no time to play. To the folks from the old country, sports always remained something utterly pagan.[38] So his parents sent him to *Atz Chaim Talmud Torah*, and his *bar mitzvah* was being planned for the following year.

The year 1929 would be a year to remember. Grandma Schprintza, at the age of seventy-three, came by ship to this country from Kalush, Poland, to see the family and attend two *simchas* (happy occasions), Dottie's wedding and Oscar's bar mitzvah.

The festivities were beginning. Family pictures were taken of the entire Schussler family, including Samson's brothers, and Mary's husband Sol and their daughter Rhoda. Schprintza, wanting to be fair to all of her children, stayed a few weeks at each of her son's apartments or homes. Some considered this cute little old lady a terror, because she argued with everyone who did not positively respond to her European ways. Maybe the children determined that two weeks was enough with each family.

Meanwhile, Harry Bregman's father started dictating terms of the wedding to Samson. "Let's wait until your brother comes to this country, and he'll help pay for the wedding."

This kind of remark did not sit well with Samson, and when Harry called Dottie a "gold digger," Samson cancelled the wedding. All of the trinkets Dottie had received were returned, and she was one very sad young lady.

Her cousin and good friend, Seymour, felt bad and tried to get her to date other men of his age. He was going to The City College of New York and also working as credit investigator for John Mullins, an installment furniture company in Brooklyn. He knew many eligible young men, but Dottie was very down on herself and refused to date. So Seymour resorted to a bit of chicanery. He belonged to a club by the name of Callagatus, which was made up of City College students. He invited her to a party, the last party of the 1929 spring term.[39]

THE CALLAGATUS CLUB MET in a basement near the school. The grey painted, windowless room was small and L-shaped and located right next to the boiler room. To get there, you had to walk down to the basement, around a corner, and down a long corridor. The only toilet, which had a hook and eye as its lock, was located at the far end of the boiler room that was lit by a cheap, porcelain, pull-chain light fixture holding a very dusty sixty-watt bulb.

The furniture in the meeting place was used but adequate, and the lights were dim. There was an old record player with an old needle and scratched records, and it had no record changer, so that records had to be put on one at a time.

The guys invited a girl's club to join them on Saturday night, June 8, as the last dance party of the year. It was to this party that Seymour invited Dottie.

The night of the party was cloudy and drizzling. With no stars or moon to light up the sky, it was particularly dark and dreary. Five thousand taxis went onto the streets that week, and with the independent drivers fixing the rate of the first mile at twenty cents, it was too expensive to take a cab. After leaving the subway station, Seymour and Dottie started the five-block walk to the clubhouse. The lights on the clubhouse street were not working. As they walked, they heard footsteps behind them and unconsciously started to walk faster. The footsteps sounded like they were running now, so they started to run. All of a sudden, a voice bellowed out, STOP! Seymour and Dottie's tightly clasped hands turned white at the knuckles, and they were frozen to the spot, too frightened to move or speak.

The Schussler Family (1922)
Top: Mary, Perl (Pepi or Mama), Samson (Papa), Dottie
Bottom: Etta, Charles (on stool), Mildred, Artie

Papa and Mama (1924)

Top: Dottie, Papa, Mama
Bottom: Etta, Mildred (1924)

Dottie in a rowboat (1927)

Seymour Schussler

The Schussler Family (June 1928)
Top: Mildred, Max, Mary & Sol Pickholz, Seymour, Oscar
Middle: Dottie, Papa (Sam), Annette, Mama (Pepi),
Rhoda Pickholz, Schprintza, Ruchal, Joseph, Fay
Bottom: Artie, Charles, Sylvia, Etta, Charlie
Schprintza (age 73) is the mother of Sam, Joseph, Oscar,
Max, and (not shown) Schmiel, Leitcha, and Jacob

4

The Meeting

There were twenty-one well-dressed young men at the clubhouse,[40] all of them wearing jackets and ties and well polished shoes. These men were an elite group. They were not wealthy but were all very intelligent and had promising future careers. The most popular member of the club, always a junior or senior, extended an invitation to a sorority, so that one telephone call guaranteed a commitment of fifteen to twenty girls.

The young ladies in the nearby all-girls schools, like Barnard, knew the potential of these most eligible bachelors and always looked forward to their socials. The other young women were there by personal invitation only.

Many of the men arrived at the basement apartment an hour before the girls in order to get the room ready for the year's final party—a party they called, "The Last Dance." There were three committees made up of volunteers who were responsible for the preparation. Those who brought their own dates were never on one of the committees that did the last minute work. The club always left cleanup for the following Monday, after classes.

Some of the fellows were in charge of food and had the responsibility to bring snacks and drinks. Although there was one bottle of scotch hidden in the cabinet behind the stored seventy-eight rpm records, only one couple indulged, the same couple observed necking in the shadows of the boiler room and who soon left the party. Someone said the fellow dropped out of school, married the following year, and left town with his wife and daughter.

All the other beverages were of the nonalcoholic type, and each one was left standing on a napkin on the top of the credenza alongside the pretzels, peanuts, and other snacks. That committee also purchased the paper napkins that were placed next to the washed glasses the club had inherited from one of the members' parents.

Another committee was in charge of entertainment. They had borrowed some phonograph records from parents and friends and stacked them vertically in a record grill. Being engineering students, they had arranged the records in alphabetical order so that any title could be found without fumbling through them all. They had also been commissioned to obtain a new record needle, donated by a parent, so that the songs would not sound scratchy and they wouldn't further damage the records.

On the week of The Last Dance, after the club's weekly meeting on Thursday evening, the four men on the committee in charge of cleaning and decorating dusted all the furniture and washed the linoleum floor. They carefully took down the streamers from the last party and rolled them to their original shape, purchased one or two more rolls and hung them strategically. The ceiling height was only seven feet, so the streamers had to be placed in such a way that from any place in the room you would have streamers over your head, but just high enough so they would not touch anyone. The forecast for the coming Saturday, the day of the dance, was rain, so they installed a pole in the boiler room for wet coats and umbrellas. The pole itself was an old broom handle that was cleverly hung horizontally from the ceiling by a piece of rope from each end.

AT LAST, SATURDAY CAME, and the committee returned to finish up. By nine o'clock, the room was ready, and the girls started to arrive at ten minutes after nine. They could have arrived earlier, but it was not considered chic to come on time. A girl was considered anxious if she was ready for a date or came to a party at the scheduled hour.

Since tonight, Seymour Schussler was bringing a lady friend—albeit his cousin—he was not required, nor did he volunteer, to serve on any committee. Seymour had to travel to Dottie's, who lived in a ground floor apartment at 1020 Forty-fifth Street in Brooklyn with her three sisters and two brothers. They took the subway to the dance; it only cost a nickel each. She looked beautiful in a summer-wear coral chiffon frock with short sleeves and cape-like collar that draped over her shoulders. The outfit came with a narrow belt that culminated in a small bow in front. White, semi-high heels and matching purse made every young man look twice.

David Weinberg, too, was an invited guest that night. Financial conditions compelled him to work, because his father, Nathan, was not a very successful man, either socially or economically. When Nathan arrived in this country in 1908, his oldest sister, Jennie, who sponsored him, helped him open a shoe repair shop. After struggling for many years, he finally ended up collecting, buying and selling junk, earning just enough to pay the rent and put food on the table. So Dave had to go out on his own and support himself. He hungered for a college education, something his father and older brother, Irving, did not have.

Work was not easy to come by for a young man in the late 1920s. The depression was starting in full swing and the white and blue-collar workers were finding it very difficult getting jobs. Only those who were exceptional with their hands or minds found employment. All the others found themselves in the unemployment lines.

Dave was exceptional in that he had an intuitive and naturally creative mind. He had attended classes at Cooper Union College, which was one of the finest architectural and engineering schools in that era. Here he met another architectural student by the name of Morris Brody who eventually became a registered architect, and together, they forged a very close friendship and mutual admiration.

Dave had found that it was just too difficult to go to school full-time and also earn a living. But he was always hungry for knowledge, and that drove him to returning to different schools to continually acquire the missing pieces that would advance his professional knowledge. He regularly put part of his wages to the advancement of his career and attended such professional schools as Pratt Institute, New York University, The Institute of Design and Construction, and The City College of New York.

While doing this, he was able to hold down some odd jobs to support a lifestyle that included friends and a car—a car being something that none of his friends had.

Henry Puchall & Company was an architectural and construction firm whose growing pains demanded that a new man be hired. This man must be capable of creating innovative and cost-effective design, and be able to gain approvals from the New York City Building Department. So, in early 1929, they hired Dave from among dozens of applicants, and gave him the title of architectural draftsman.

Dave called this job "The School of Hard Knocks." He learned the ropes of getting approvals of plans and specifications; whom to see and how to compromise design criteria in order to get his company's plans approved. He made many friends in the department, from the examiners all the way up to the commissioner. These were good business relationships that grew into friendships. If any of his new friends needed a favor, he would always be there to offer his services—free. And thus was born the expression, "I wash your hands, and you wash mine." Because of this, Dave never had any problems getting his plans approved; these close relationships would be instrumental in his future success.

DAVE HAD DECIDED NOT to go to The Last Dance because he worked that Saturday, but his friend Seymour had prevailed upon him to come, saying that it was the last party of the school year. So reluctantly, Dave had agreed.

He took his car to work that morning, wanting to drive to the clubhouse that night. Because the club was located in a residential neighborhood, he had to park several blocks away. The weather wasn't particularly nice that evening, so he walked fast to arrive at the party before it started to rain.

It was quite a coincidence that he saw Seymour walking toward the clubhouse, holding hands with a girl, so he increased his pace to catch up with them. It was dark because some of the streetlights were not working, and it seemed as if the faster he walked, the faster Seymour and the girl would walk. So he started to run. When Dave started to run, *they* started to run. How ironic, how ridiculous! So he yelled for them to STOP!

When he finally caught up to them, they appeared scared to death. Seymour explained why they were so frightened, and they all had a good laugh. Then Seymour introduced his cousin Dottie to his good friend Dave, and they all proceeded to the party together.

The chance meeting in the street, and the laughs they had on the way to the clubroom, cemented an early friendship. The other young men there that night tried to get to know Dottie, but she was already enthralled with Dave. He was an extremely shy young man, and she had a good time enticing him to talk about himself. After a night of constant chatter, Dave gave Dottie and Seymour a ride, dropping her off first. Taking Seymour home, Dave told him that she was a lovely girl whom he would like to know better. But he was not going to call her now because he was not secure in his job, and he needed to complete his education.

Seymour had other ideas.

IT APPEARED TO PAPA THAT his daughter Dottie had been in a depressed mood since breaking up with her fiancé, Harry. Since Oscar's bar mitzvah in February, her depression was getting worse. Harry had called her a "gold digger," and despite her knowing it wasn't true, she felt stigmatized. Her father, a bright man, did not want her to sit around and do nothing, getting further down on herself. In that state of mind, it would be much more difficult for her to find a man. She needed to clear her thoughts of fairytale fiction. So he decided to take her for a walk and talk.

After work on Monday, Seymour called Dottie, and she told him that she was going for a walk with her father on the boardwalk at Coney Island. Her best friends, Mable Pollack and Rose Braunstein were busy studying, and Papa had come home wanting to cool off after a day in the "sweat shop," and said, "Let's go to Coney Island." So Mama was going to stay home to take care of the children, and she and Papa would go. This was Seymour's opportunity. He was going to strike while the proverbial iron was hot.

He called Dave and asked him if he felt like taking a ride to Coney Island. It was a warm, muggy night, and Coney Island was the perfect place to cool off. Dave was not prepared for what was about to happen to him.

Dottie, who always was into the latest fashions, wore a sudanette—an exquisite, sleeveless cotton shirting, beautifully lustrous, impeccably detailed, with a high back and a bow above the cleavage line. She wore flat shoes and a small, tight-fitting hat called a baku. She looked beautiful.

They hadn't been walking but half an hour, when a pair of hands reached around her from behind and covered her eyes.[41]

"Guess who?" a voice said.

Dottie knew the voice very well. It was her cousin, Seymour.

For the next hour, Seymour, Dave, Dottie, and Papa had a nice chat while strolling the boardwalk. Seymour engaged Papa in conversation and their gait slowed so Dottie and Dave were walking ahead and alone.

Back home, Papa would tell Mama, for all to hear, that Dottie met a young man who looks like a nice fellow.

For David Weinberg, June 10, 1929, was a memorable night. His heart had been pierced with the arrow of Cupid. The remainder of the summer and on through December of that year was a whirlwind romance.

Isn't it ironic, that a day exactly sixty-four years afterward was to be, for me, equally memorable? Between that one day and the other lies the rest of this book.

David (1924)

David

The Weinberg Family (circa 1918)
Top: Gladys, Frances, Irving, Annie (Hinde or The Ma), David
Bottom: Nathan (Natan or The Pa), Mac

5

The Early Years

HE WAS GANGLY. At five foot seven inches in height, he weighed all of 130 pounds. When he took his shirt off, he looked like a skeleton in skin. Tall, dark, and handsome were not the adjectives others used to describe him. However, he was polite, always well dressed and very well groomed. With clean, sharply pressed garments, highly polished shoes, clean fingernails, and a clean-shaven face, he looked sharp. He had blue eyes shaded behind dark-rimmed glasses and fluffy, light brown hair anointed with olive oil to keep it down and neatly combed to the sides. His fingers were long and stained by nicotine.

David, called Dave by his contemporaries, smoked cigarettes for a reason. If he were asked a question and needed time to formulate a response, he took a deep puff to allow him to think of an answer.

Dave had a thirst for knowledge hampered only by lack of money. His father, Nathan, was a poor man who worked day-to-day to pay the rent and feed and clothe his family. After his children had achieved the minimal education required by law, he had shipped them off to work so they could support themselves and help support "The Ma" and "The Pa," the names by which their children referred to them. All of the children had gone to public school in Brooklyn, and Dave had gone to Public School 168 and graduated at the age of fourteen.

The processional song at that graduation was "Are You for Me, Or Against Me?" The principal, Robert Frost, addressed the predominantly Jewish graduates by reading from the Scriptures, and the Honorable David H. Moore, chairman of the local school board, saluted the graduates and distributed the diplomas.[42] Wednesday, June 23, 1920, was a memorable day in young David's life. He was a bright lad, and the messages he received from the platform, to rise to the highest educational level, were etched in his mind forever.

His older brother, Irving, upon high school graduation, had become a delivery boy. Frances, the second child, born two years after Irving and two years before Dave, had gone to Girls High School. Both Irving and Frances had been born in what was called "The Old Country," Lodz, Poland. The *Pa* had sent Frances to Girls High to learn typing so she could make more money as an executive secretary than could the smart girls who went on to become teachers. Even Dave's sister Gladys, two years his junior, went to secretarial school where she learned not only to type, but also how to take shorthand. She was smart, beautiful, provocative, and so proficient that she eventually became secretary to John H. Shaw, consul general of Ethiopia.[43]

Dave, wanting an education of higher learning, went to Commercial High School in Brooklyn and was immediately recognized by his peers as an intellect, albeit a very shy and retiring one. By his third year in high school, he had been elected to The Arista, a service and scholarship organization that recognized the intellectual elite of the school.[44] He remained a member of Arista until his graduation in 1924. The senior book, called the *Senior Ledger*, June 1924, lists his salient services as a member of Arista, a marshal, and office assistant. *The Senior Knock*, indicating an underlying trait, said that David "wants to be a traffic cop on a desert island!"[45]

The Weinberg family was not what one would call "close-knit." No one among them liked anyone else. The Pa was the king. The children knew what he said was law. He was extremely strict, and he was fast to remove his belt and use it on the rear end of the disobedient child. Even Dave's mother, Annie, knew that The Pa was the ruler, and that she was only in charge of the kitchen. She was a sweet lady who listened and reacted to what went on around her. With the help of her girls, she made the meals and cleaned the house. If she did wrong in the eyes of The Pa, he would not speak to her for days and sometimes weeks, until *she* apologized.

Fierce sibling rivalry and the feeling that the man is the ruler, stood between the second born child, Frances and her older brother, Irving. Irving seldom treated Frances well. He felt that after The Pa, he should be the family's ruling authority.[46]

Dave and Irving slept in the same bed. Because he was four years younger, Dave would be the first to go to sleep. Irving did not want Dave in the bed because he felt it was too small for the two of them, so when Irving went to bed, he would kick Dave onto the floor, and there Dave would often sleep. This was repeated several times a night for several years, until Dave became old enough to fend for himself. The Pa never intervened.

The two girls, Frances and Gladys, had chores in the house, but the boys were exempt from cleaning, washing, and dusting, as well as from any kitchen chores. That did not sit right with the girls, and they resented their brothers.

Gladys, who was four years younger than Frances, felt that her older sister took advantage of her. They just didn't trust each other. It seemed to each that she was always doing most of the house chores. Come the religious holidays, it was Gladys who made the *gefilte* fish, a habit that continued into her marriage. Gladys also said she was the one who helped her mother with all the holiday preparations.

Although the family was religious and observed some of the Jewish holidays, they did not follow all the rituals. On Yom Kippur, they fasted. On Passover, they had a Seder. But, despite the fact that the boys went to Hebrew School, they did not strictly follow the faith.

The six of them were cramped into the small apartment at 548 Flushing Avenue in Brooklyn.[47] Space was even tighter when the fifth and last child, Max, was born in 1913. They moved to 614 Broadway in Brooklyn,[48] a move that allowed Frances to complete elementary school and start Girls High School at the lowest level. Dave had two more years in his new elementary school, and Max was starting kindergarten. The timing was right. All the kids loved Max, called *Mac* by his brothers and sisters, and he became the glue that eventually held the family together.

After his graduation from high school, Dave had to help support the family, but he still hungered for a degree in architecture. He got himself a job so he could contribute to the family income, a self-imposed obligation that he continued when Nathan went blind and could no longer support himself. At last, Dave convinced his two brothers to help, and they all shared the burden. They never asked the girls, and the girls never offered to help, because they all felt it was a man's obligation to help the parents survive.

So Dave went in and out of college for the next few years, gaining an education and still helping to support his parents.

In June of 1927, before he turned twenty-five, Irving married Maime Goldstein. In August of 1928, their first son, Marvin, was born.

In 1928, Dave's younger sister, Gladys, at the age of twenty, married Irwin Baum and she gave birth to a son, Myron, in January of 1929.

Until this time, Dave had not even been aware that girls existed. He was interested in getting an education and making money so he could live a better life than his parents had. That is, until he met and befriended a fellow by the name of Seymour Schussler, Dottie's cousin, who was a student at the City College of New York, a member of a club called Callagatus.

AFTER THE CHANCE MEETING with Dottie and her father on the boardwalk at Coney Island on June 10, 1929, Dave didn't know what hit him. All he thought about was Dottie, and he began to see her more and more frequently. The ten-cent movies and a fifteen-cent ice cream soda, a drive to Coney Island for a five-cent hot dog at Nathan's, dinner at a nice restaurant, or gatherings at either his or her friends' apartments became weekly events. Though up until this, never one to own a calendar, he now wrote down the time of every date and where they were to spend the day or evening.

So it wasn't surprising that he entered on his calendar the most important day of his young life. It was at 7 PM on December 29, 1929, that David Weinberg and Dorothy Schussler became engaged. It was such a memorable event that he kept that page of the calendar with their engagement picture for posterity.[49]

The next year was a whirlwind for Dave and Dottie. She was preparing for the wedding. Dottie had to not only get her gown, but also to find a reception hall that was within the budget imposed by her parents' thin wallet, make up the guest list, arrange for the flowers, the band, the food, and everything else involved in joining hands with the person with whom she would spend the rest of her life.

Dottie's sixteen-year-old sister Mildred said that Dave was so straight, that when Dottie went out of town to a wedding, he spent the evening with her so Dottie would know he wasn't with anyone else.[50]

Dave had to make sure that he had a job that would fulfill the requirements of a good husband and a providing father. In early 1930, he left his position at one company to take on additional responsibilities and get a better salary with the architectural and construction firm of Henry Puchall & Company.

And so it went for the next nine months.

DOTTIE HAD BEEN RAISED in a very religious environment, and her mother, Pepi, had guided her in performing proper female rituals. Jewish parents would do anything to provide their children with physical, mental, and spiritual health. What sacrifices would they not be willing to endure to assure their child the physical and moral fiber that would enable them to fight impurity? This was not only the *job* of a Jewish parent, but an *obligation*.[51]

Pepi told her children that the Torah says you should, "Sanctify yourself so that you may be holy."[52] It continues to command that, having made yourself holy, you rise above the morass of animal instincts. Discipline your desires. Then you will ascend from the lowly level of the animal to the standard of man as he was truly meant to be. The laws of the Holy Scripture are in perfect harmony with hygiene. The bride and mother to be must be clean and *kosher* for the children to be healthy.

These laws brought forth the requirements of immersion in a *mikvah*. A small pool of water constructed and filled according to the precise requirements of Jewish law, a mikvah looks like a miniature swimming pool. The tiled area is about eight feet square, and the pool is about five feet square and four feet deep. The water surface is about three feet below the level in which you enter. There is a tiled stair with a stainless steel handrail that leads down to the pool. The waters in the mikvah are "living waters" that must come directly from natural sources. It is usually rain water that comes off a surface, such as the roof, and is allowed to flow into a cistern used as a holding tank inside the building, allowing the water to warm to the inside temperature.

Mama had gone to mikvah every month of her adult life and implored her three eldest daughters to go. She would tell them that she had carried them with great delight right next to her heart and raised them in happiness despite the many hardships, struggles, and suffering, until the Good Lord, with His loving-kindness, had brought them to the happiest moment of their lives. She would say to each of them, "Now, after all the motherly fears and anxieties, you have reached the joyful day of your wedding. For all I have sacrificed on your behalf, I ask one thing in return. Fulfill the duties and responsibilities of a truly Jewish daughter. Preserve our family's traditional purity according to the Torah. Do not destroy our family tree with sacrilegious hands." She would conclude by making this appeal, "… with the assurance that the Creator will send rewards of His bountiful blessings for you, your husband, and your children."

And so, two nights before the wedding, Dottie went to the mikvah. First she followed all the rituals of cleaning every part of her body in a bathtub of warm water, clipping and cleaning her nails, and scrubbing her hair. In the mikvah, she immersed once, said the prayer, and immersed two more times. She was now ready for the wedding.

THE HURRICANE IN THE CARIBBEAN that hit the Dominican Republic on September 5, causing the deaths of twelve hundred people, was threatening to come north toward New York. Although the temperature on the day of the wedding reached a high of seventy-three degrees, the effects of the hurricane brought showers to the New York area.[53] But in Jewish folklore, rain is a good omen.

September 6, 1930, was the day when Dorothy and David were united in wedded bliss, and two souls were reunited. According to the *Zohar*, the central book in Jewish mystical tradition, each soul, prior to its entry into the world, consists of male and female united into one being. When the soul descends on earth, at birth, the two parts separate and animate two different bodies. These individual souls spend their entire earthly life looking for their original mate: the other half that was separated from them prior to birth. When the time for marriage arrives, the Holy Blessed One, who knows all souls, unites them again as they were before. Thus, they once again constitute one body and one soul, forming the right and the left side of one individual.[54]

The men in the wedding party wore tuxedos, and the women wore similar white dresses. Dottie's older married sister, Mary Pickholz, was the matron of honor, her younger sister, Mildred, was the maid of honor and the flower girls included her younger sisters, Yetta and Annette and her niece, Rhoda Pickholz. Mac, Dave's seventeen-year-old brother, was the best man.[55]

Some of the other people in the wedding party were Dave's friends, Charley Fine, Jules Cohen, Harry Liebowitz, and cousins Sam Steg and Seymour Schussler who was Dave's friend and Dottie's cousin—the same Seymour who introduced them the year before. The ladies included friends Elsie Marcus, Gussie Saposnick, Lee Saperstein, and Ray Bitterman. Dave's older sister, Frances, and cousin Rose Steg rounded out the group.

Rabbi Morris Rose presided over the wedding ceremony.[56] He was the first one down the aisle, followed by the wedding attendants and ushers. Next came Nathan and Annie, one on either side of Dave, who was wearing a black tuxedo adorned with flowers on the left lapel. They walked to the *chuppah*, made up of four poles and decorated across the top and two sides with flowers. The chuppah, required by the Talmud for marriage, symbolizes the groom's home and the bride's new domain.[57] So, Dave—the only one to stand under the chuppah; all the others were standing outside looking in—awaited his bride. He wore a white bow tie with his white shirt, and as usual, he was impeccably groomed, with his light brown hair parted on the left side and his mustache very neatly trimmed.

Mama and Papa walked down the aisle with Dottie between them. She wore a white wedding gown with a four foot sheer white train. A floral lace veil with simple but elegant flowers that were secured to the dress covered her face. Two-foot-long white ribbon laces were interspersed with the floral bouquet that was made up of different colored roses and ferns. A soft, pretty smile was on her lips. She was a beautiful bride.

Half way down the aisle, Mama and Papa raised Dottie's veil, placed a kiss on each cheek and proceeded to the *bema*—the altar—to stand on the opposite side of the chuppah facing Nathan and Annie. Dave then left the chuppah and went to escort his bride back with him. As the rabbi chanted the introductory prayers,

Dottie walked around Dave seven times. This custom is of Kabbalistic origin[58] and has had several interpretations, from representing the earth's seven revolutions during the seven days of creation to the protective circle for thwarting the malicious designs of any demons who are jealous of the happiness of the bride and groom.

Before placing the ring on Dottie's finger, Dave recited the marriage proposal in both Hebrew and English. The proposal was, "Behold, thou art betrothed unto me, with this ring, in accordance with the Law of Moses and Israel." The ring, too, appears to be of ancient tradition, since there is no reference to it in the Talmud.

The most important part of the ceremony is the reading and the signing of the *ketubah*. The ketubah—which literally means, "that which is written"—is the contract that the man makes with his wife, declaring his obligations as a husband according to the Jewish law and custom and the penalties to which he agrees if he does not carry out those obligations.

The rabbi then recited the seven benedictions—*Sheva Berakhot*—starting with the blessing over the wine and culminating with the blessing of joy, pleasure, love and peace that will assist the bridegroom to rejoice with the bride.

The end of the ceremony was marked by the long awaited custom of breaking the glass, which was wrapped in a cloth to contain the shards. There are many reasons offered for this custom. One is derived from Psalm 2:11, which says, "Serve the Lord with fear and rejoice with trembling." Another is that it represents the destruction of the ancient temple in Jerusalem in the first century. The glass was smashed under the foot of the groom, after which everyone said, "*Mazel tov*"—Good luck.

Then it was all music and dancing to a five-piece band for four hours while partaking of food. They danced the foxtrot, waltz, the Jewish *hora*, the Russian *kazatske*, and a Hungarian dance called the *czardas*—pronounced shardosh.[59] The czardas is danced by couples, with the man holding his partner's waist and the girl holding the man's shoulders. During this dance, the partners lean with their weight away from each other and swing each other vigorously. Although Dave danced with his new bride, or shall we say, held onto his new bride for dear life, he felt very awkward. Dave had the proverbial, two left feet. He not only did not know any of the dance routines, he couldn't even hear a drum beat. But he was always a good sport and danced to the kidding of his friends. The flowers were beautiful, the food was wonderful, and the music set the happy mood. It was a *frelach*—a happy—affair, and the bride and groom made a beautiful couple.

They spent their one-week honeymoon in upstate New York, in a small town called Dairyland.

DAVE CONTINUED TO DO VERY WELL at Puchall & Company and was receiving periodic raises. So the couple moved from their first temporary apartment on Linden Boulevard and Church Avenue to a small apartment at 926 Forty-seventh Street in Brooklyn where they stayed until a few months prior to the birth of their first child. With another raise, they were able to move to a nice apartment building at 1621 Sixty-fifth Street[60] where they lived for the next three years.

Jews in the early third of the century usually followed the tradition of their parents and siblings. It was felt that fruitfulness in marriage was a great blessing and childlessness a tragedy and disgrace.[61] Even in the Bible it is written that the purposes of marriage are companionship and procreation. "It is not good that the man should be alone. A man shall leave his father and mother and shall cleave unto his wife and they shall be one flesh."[62]

Dorothy's parents had married and had their first child in less than nine months. David's parents had their first child in the first nine months, both following the traditions of their forefathers. And so, nine months later, on Saturday, June 20, 1931, Dottie gave her husband a Father's Day gift of their first son, Martin, named after Dave's father's father, Moishe. Martin's birth was during a continuing heat wave when daytime temperatures reached eighty-five degrees. The upper deck of the Manhattan Bridge, which had opened two days earlier, had traffic jams that lasted four hours. This was the year that Herbert Hoover's 1932 reelection campaign got underway. In those days, Dave smoked Chesterfield cigarettes whose ad said, "Smokers want a milder cigarette. Chesterfields is just that. It is smoked by more men and women every day." Beech-Nut Gum jumped on the smoking bandwagon and proclaimed, "Chewing Beech-Nut Gum makes smoking more enjoyable." Wanamakers was selling men's fine suits for $39.50, Panama hats for $3.95, Oxford shoes for $4.90, and women's dresses for $3.95.[63]

As easygoing as Dottie was, Dave was extremely strict and ruled the house with an iron hand. When he said No, that was the law. He was very stubborn. When he was wrong, he was still right.[64] Dottie was very happy to stay home and nurture her son. When they went shopping for clothes, Dave went along for the drive and to pay the bills, but it was Dottie who made the selections. Dave was a strict disciplinarian. If Martin was disobedient, he would feel "the wrath of Dave." There was no such thing as a "play date" at that time, so Marty grew up deprived of an early intermingling with other children his age. Looking back, he says that he did not have many friends. "This might have to do with how I was dressed, how I was brought up, and how I behaved."

It was on January 25, 1941, that Dr. Seckler, the family doctor, diagnosed Martin with Saint Vitus's dance. The illness was a childhood disease of the nervous system, possibly caused by streptococci, manifested by spasmodic movements of the body.[65] He questions to this day if it was the effect of his strict upbringing.[66]

It was important to the young parents to have a time away from the chores of the apartment, so every summer, they took a room in a Catskill Mountain resort called the Pearl Lake Hotel. It was there they met Irene and George Burch, with whom they made a very lasting friendship. Dottie would stay at the hotel with Martin during the week and spend most of her time with Irene. The husbands would come up to the mountains on the weekends and the couples would be inseparable. Their friendship forged in the mid 1930s was unbreakable; they continued to socialize all year, every year, for the rest of their lives.

In the course of the next ten years, several other couples joined the circle, and they became a very close-knit group. In addition to the Weinbergs and Burchs, there were Sam and Jeanne Berliner, Jack and Terry Keller, and Ben and Judy Silbert. There were two or three others who occasionally joined for short periods, but these five couples always stayed together. As time went on, Dottie would invite her sisters and their spouses to join the fun. On September 7, 1935, exactly five years and a day after Dottie married Dave, her sister Mildred married Sid Kalikow, and in 1942, her sister Etta married Milton Salant. There were times when one or both of those two couples joined the group.

For several years, business in general had been declining. Building owners could not hold onto properties because of lack of funds, and design and construction work virtually ceased. In 1935, things were not going well for the Puchall Company, and in early October, Dave lost his job. But on October 14, 1935, John (Jack) Westney, with the Bank for Savings, interviewed and immediately offered him a job for one month as a temporary architectural draftsman. There was no choice, so Dave accepted. This was a time when the bank was foreclosing and repossessing quite a number of properties and then wondering what in the world to do with them. So the bank had Dave visit the properties, sketch their physical dimensions, and draw up plans and specifications for renovations.[67] There were several problems, though.

One major problem: Dave was a Jew. The bank couldn't have a Jew as a department head. He was the token in an organization of white Anglo-Saxon Protestants who couldn't stand the fact that a Jew was more informed about something than they were. That was the fact. He was more knowledgeable than anyone at the bank about design, approval, and construction. The only way they could keep the Jew away from them was to keep him employed as a "temporary" and keep him out of the dining room. But they eventually offered him a deal. If he would change his name, they would recommend that he be given "permanent status." He refused. So he had to eat at the more expensive diners around the corner on Sixteenth Street. They also kept him at arm's length by giving him the "dirty" work of going to the filthy, dilapidated buildings by himself and doing the inspections and the measuring. They knew this was a Herculean task for one man, but Dave would successfully develop methods of measuring and sketching by himself.[68]

The next problem was that Dave did not have a State of New York license to practice architecture. So the bank hired Louis Ordwein, but, as with most architects at that time, there was nothing for him to design and build. So he was thrilled to get this job as the bank's architect.

Taking a tenement and converting it to apartments required a very special knowledge and understanding of how it should be accomplished, and the bank had picked the right man. With Dave as Ordwein's leg, idea, and drawing man, the plans started to flow out of the office with regularity. That created another problem for the bank. They sent their "building department" team to get New York City approval, and found that most of the time, the city turned them down. Of course the blame for the bad design strategies was thrown to Dave.

In an effort to embarrass him and take the proverbial "heat" off of themselves, the officers told the bank president that Dave should be sent to the Building Department to obtain approval for his ridiculous ideas and plans. They wanted the Jew fired. But Dave always returned from the Municipal Building with approval for his plans. Need one say that the officers were embarrassed and the bank president impressed? With every disapproval that the "team" received, Dave went right back and got the approval. The bank president decided to eliminate the position of building department team and create the job of building department liaison and give it Architectural Draftsman Dave Weinberg.

Meanwhile, Dottie's mother was not well. Pepi Schussler had had a hard life. She had given birth to nine children in twenty years, two of whom died at a very young age. She was sweet and loving, and a very good role model for her older children. Her younger children were too young to appreciate how hard she worked in the house and how she struggled to make ends meet. Her greatest joy had been to see her three oldest daughters married. But on the morning of

December 18, 1935, her heart gave out. It was Shabbos and the eighth day of *Chanukah*.[69] Her son Oscar (now called Artie), then age nineteen, remembers running through the snow to bring a doctor to the house. It was too late.

MAMA WAS BURIED THE NEXT DAY, and Dottie was devastated. The period of mourning, called "*shivah*," was seven days, starting from the day of the burial. The Hebrew word means seven. The shivah took place at Samson's home where all the children gathered everyday. The girls did not use any makeup and the boys did not shave. They did not wear leather shoes, listen to the radio, or engage in any pleasures. Mirrors, symbols of vanity as well as distractions, were covered during shivah. They all sat on low, hard-surfaced stools or boxes. At the conclusion of shivah, the family took a walk around the block, another symbolic way of showing the end of mourning and a return to normal living.

Dottie was hit hard by the loss of her beloved mother. She had periods of melancholy that dragged on for weeks and months, in which she would sit and cry at her loss. Mama had been her best friend, and nothing and no one was able to console her. And no one was able to take the place of Mama.

But one night, Dottie had a dream. There would be someone who would replace the emptiness created when Mama died. It was time to have another child and have that child named after her mother. So it was back to the mikvah in early March.

She conceived quickly and gave birth eight months later to a son, Paul—the author of this book. Born on November 9, 1936, I was the first descendant to be named after Perl Schussler.

The *Briss*, or circumcision—the rite of removing the foreskin from the penis by surgical means—was held at the hospital on November 16, 1936, eight days after birth. In attendance were Dave, Dorothy, and Martin, as well as Dave's parents and cousin and Dottie's father, her sister Mary, with husband Sol and children Rhoda and Jerome, and sister Mildred with husband Sid. Mildred and Sid were chosen as the Godmother and the Godfather. Dave's father, Nathan, held the baby during the procedure and was called the *sandik*—the child's patron. There were many other friends and relatives in attendance; twenty-eight people in all.[70]

At this time, they were living at 874 Forty-third Street in Brooklyn.[71] With the addition of a second child and Martin ready to start first grade, they made another move, to 9 Webster Avenue, Brooklyn. There, you could hear the faint rumble of the Culver Line trains running over the trolley tracks on McDonald Avenue, one block east. This larger two-bedroom apartment was across the street from the elementary school, P.S. 192. Martin would start first grade in September of 1937, and then attend Montauk Junior High School, just under one half mile away. At that time, it was considered within walking distance. Although moving frequently had seemed in style for the Weinbergs, they would live at this address for the next seventeen years.

But a threatening cloud passed over. It was the cloud that carried the memory of Dottie's young sister, Evelyn, who died at the age of six, eighteen years earlier, in the 1918 Influenza Epidemic. Dottie had never forgotten that tragedy, and now the country was in the agony of a pneumonia crisis. Pneumonia was one of the leading causes of death in the United States,[72] and her two-week-old son, Paul, had a case affecting both of his lungs—double Pneumonia.

Pneumonia, a lung disease involving inflammation resulting from viral or bacterial infection, was claiming one third of its victims.[73] It was a seasonal disease that took place in the colder months. So this was the worst time of the year to get the illness.[74] Dottie sat vigil for seven days and nights, making sure Paul got all the care needed for him to survive. The crisis passed, and the exhausted but relieved Dottie had a son who would be the living image of her mother.

Dottie's friends said that the sun shone when Paul walked in. He was always happy and friendly to everyone and had a smile for anyone who held him. Irene Burch was not the only one who said that Paul was her baby. Dottie glowed and felt that her life was renewed.

So the author of this book was born, was alive, and finally was well.

DAVE'S TEMPORARY STATUS at the bank continued. Manpower, however, was becoming short due to the impending war. Dave's reputation for efficiency and getting difficult situations resolved quickly had spread, and he was offered work at other institutions. However, he felt a debt of gratitude to the bank president for the trust he had showed in him. So Dave told the president that he would stay if the "temporary" part of his title was dropped and he was given full privileges. In 1940, David Weinberg became a "permanent" employee of the Bank for Savings with full dining room privileges.

The bank had just hired Alfred Mills and Dolsen Rausher from the Prudential Insurance Company to supervise the mortgage department. Alfred Mills soon became the next chairman of the board and president of the bank, and Rauscher took charge of the mortgage department. Then the bank entered a new phase of construction. They were acquiring office buildings, and Dave became involved with the planning and alteration of office space, both for rent and for sale. It was shortly thereafter that the Bank for Savings merged with the New York Savings

Bank and the merged organization became known as the New York Bank for Savings.

Dave was immediately given the added responsibilities of dealing with the contractors and the foremen on the job. His leadership led to quick approvals at the Building Department, "fast turnaround" construction, all resulting in very profitable sales of many properties that did not look anywhere near like what they had when they were repossessed.

THE SECOND WORLD WAR had begun. As the married father of two children and above the age of conscription, Dave was not inducted into the armed services as was his younger brother and Dottie's two brothers. However, he did his national duty by becoming an air raid warden. As soon as the air raid alarm was sounded, he donned his official hard hat and began patrolling the streets insuring all lights in residences on Webster Avenue were turned off. The top half of automobile headlights had to be painted black, and when the siren sounded, most cars stopped and lights were turned off. As good citizens, the Weinbergs purchased war bonds to help their government wage the war against Nazi Germany and Japan.

It was 1944, and anti-Semitism was running rampant at the bank. At dinner, Dave would tell his family the events that took place daily with his pompous, hate-filled bosses, and he would share these stories with his close friends. The pressure started to have an adverse effect on his health, and his skin erupted with something that looked like hives.

The first person he consulted was the family physician, Dr. Samuel Seckler, whose office was at 320 Empire Boulevard in Brooklyn. The doctor recommended two things. The first was to consult a dermatologist, and the second was to leave it alone and watch it disappear with the same speed with which it had come. However, Dave went from doctor to doctor for a quick cure. First it was diagnosed as poison ivy, then poison sumac and then poison oak. The medications for those rashes did not work, so they gave the rash a new name, acute dermatitis. All the doctors used him as a guinea pig by giving him different salves in the attempt to eliminate the rash, which now had spread to his entire body, and to relieve the intense itch. Nothing worked. He took hot baths. He took cold baths. The itching intensified. During the night he scratched until he bled, and in the morning, the sheets were covered with blood. He started to wear gloves at night to prevent further skin damage. It did not work. He then tried boxing gloves, and he scratched right through them. He visited doctors from New York to California to Texas. They told him to try different topical medications and return the following week. Nothing worked. When the doctors learned he had no more money, they all said the same thing.

"When you find the cure, call me, and on your way out, pay the secretary."

The fee was usually in excess of $100. That they could not cure him or help him was no reason for the patient to be excused from paying the fee.

If there was any humor in all this, it was that Dottie told her sons to become dermatologists. "Dermatologists won't cure you and they won't kill you. They have regular working hours, are never awakened in the middle of the night, and they make a lot of money." Dave went to so many doctors that he ran out of money. The only relief that he got was from the dry heat of Florida and Arizona. But how much time could he spend away from his job?

When he returned to New York after a stay in Florida, the rash intensified once again. He sat in the bathtub in an oatmeal mix prescribed by yet another doctor. The itch and the pain were excruciating and debilitating. One Saturday, he was so weakened that he was unable to get out of the tub, and he lay there crying. Dottie did not have the strength to lift him. He sobbed to her, "What is the solution?"

Dottie was frantic and called their close friend Sam Berliner who rushed to the apartment and sat in the bathroom and reasoned with Dave to make him forget a little bit, and then carried him back to bed.[75] Sam was not only a big, strong, strapping man who was also very wealthy, he also idolized Dave who had done some design and consulting work for Sam and his company and had never charged him. Dave did that for all his friends, and now this was payback time. Sam gave Dave several signed blank checks and told him to fill in the amounts and not to worry about repayment.

This illness went on for ten years. It was the most devastating time of his life and the life of the family. It is interesting to note that another friend, George Burch, also offered money, but not one member of the Weinberg family, not one sibling, offered any moral, spiritual, or monetary help.

Dave was irritable most of the time. Dottie doted on his every whim and wish in order to ease the tension in his life and to make his existence—which was all his life was at that point—a bit more tolerable. To pay doctor bills, Dave had to use the money given to him by his friend, Sam. Despite his illness, he continued to work at the bank so that he would be able to earn enough to pay the expenses for the family. Their marriage wasn't yet twenty years old, and Dave was being crushed by the pressures of his illness, his job, and the financial concerns at home. It was a horrible time. He went about his work at the bank calmly and efficiently.

When he came home, he took out all his anxieties, frustrations, and pain on the family.

Martin was doing very well in school; Dave and Dottie were proud of his grades. His teachers raved about his academic performance. During Open School Week, parents were invited to attend their children's classes and quietly observe their progress. Mrs. Hinshey, Martin's second grade teacher, told Dottie to watch Martin when she asked the next question. Before she was able to get the full question asked, all the hands were raised—except for Martin's. She asked several of the students the answer, and they replied that they didn't know—obviously because the question wasn't yet asked. Mrs. Hinshey asked why they raised their hands if they didn't know the answer. When the question was asked in full, the only one with the answer was Martin.

When Paul—the author of this book—entered elementary school, he performed well but had nowhere near the academic achievements of his older brother. He loved to play ball—the only member of the Schussler descendants to love the ball game. One of his weaknesses was his inability to stay clean. The moment he left the house, it was off to the schoolyard for a punchball game, a stickball game, basketball or football game, or whatever game there was where he could get filthy. Dottie nicknamed him "Kid Schmutz," the Dirty Kid. It was a term of endearment and Paul loved it.

Despite Dave's debilitating illness, Dottie made plans for their son Paul's bar mitzvah. Before Dave became ill in 1944, Paul, at the age of seven, had begun attending the Ocean Parkway Jewish Center to get a Jewish education. Martin had attended that Hebrew school and was bar mitzvahed there in June 1944. The Center was a ten-block walk, taken three times during the week and once on Sunday morning. The sessions during the week were for reading, writing, and learning elementary conversation. On Sunday, Jewish history stories were told. Paul loved the stories and, despite his love for playing ball on Sunday, would never miss a Sunday class.

It was very important to Dottie for her boys to learn the ways of the Torah. "You're a Jew. Be proud of it. Marry a Jewish girl and carry on the tradition," she would say.

One day, Paul came home from Hebrew school and told his mother that he had met a girl named Dolores and was going to marry her. He was all of eight years of age. Dottie always knew how to handle Paul and wanted him to understand that a *shiksa*, a girl who was not Jewish, would not be acceptable. So she told him it was wonderful, but is she Jewish? When Paul said he'd met Dolores in Hebrew school, Dottie sighed and immediately said it was fine to get married.

"Of course, you must have a well paying job to support her and then give her a diamond ring." It was Paul's turn to sigh, and he said, "I think I'll put it off until next year."

It was 1947, and Paul was not attending Shabbos services in shul and *davening*—praying—with the speed and accuracy that Dottie thought was necessary. Her father, Samson, suggested getting group lessons twice a week at the temple and private lessons once a week from a rabbi of the temple nearby. The rabbi would give the lessons at the Weinberg home. So Paul took the lessons and went to services every Saturday morning for a year. His progress in reading the *Shemonah Esreh* or the *Amidah*, which is the prayer meaning "Eighteen Benedictions," and is said while standing, did improve. That prayer, one of the most sacred and solemn prayers, is read three times a day in an undertone to allow intimate communion by the worshiper with his own conscience and with his Creator. However, when Dottie found the rabbi and Paul playing chess in the bedroom, she was furious and fired the rabbi—who, by the way, never did beat the precocious kid at chess.

A year passed, and the bar mitzvah was now a year away. Samson recommended that his close friend and neighbor teach Paul the *haftorah*, a supplemental reading to the Torah, and have him ready by the appointed day. That rabbi was strict, all business. He had Paul chanting his haftorah over and over again until he did it with perfection. Paul walked a mile to his house three times a week and learned his lessons well, even though Dave and Dottie spent much of the year in Miami, Florida and in Tucson, Arizona where Dave, in the fourth year of his dreaded skin disease, was in treatment. Every week, they would call their boys to find out how they were doing.

That year, 1948, was not an easy year for Paul. In June he graduated from Public School 192 and was starting Montauk Junior High School in the very successful footsteps of his older brother. Dottie would spend many months of the year in Arizona and Florida with Dave, praying that this year would bring the cure. Dottie's sisters, Mary and Millie, tried to ease the burden on Paul by having him sleep at one of their houses several times a week and on weekends. Mary lived across the street from Montauk, and it was an easy commute to school. However, it robbed him of the camaraderie of his friends.

On top of all that, Paul continued his bar mitzvah lessons from the taskmaster rabbi. Samson was sure to criticize every error Paul made when he practiced at home. Jerome, Dottie's sister Mary's son, witnessed the verbal abuse. Samson threatened to "send you away if you don't do your work."[76] It was an extremely trying time. As young as he was, Paul felt his older brother had a superior attitude toward him, never gave him any support, all of which put another layer of pressure on the boy.

The equation was complete. Paul's parents spent much time away from the house rehabilitating Dave. Grandpa Sam said nothing positive to give Paul an emotional lift—quite the contrary—and his brother, Martin, with whom he spent most of his time, was too involved with his studies to give his kid brother, over five years his junior, an occasional pat on the back.

ALTHOUGH MARTIN WAS THE STUDIOUS ONE, Paul got all the attention from the aunts and uncles. They called him "The Personality Kid" and showered him with lots of love and attention, (which I graciously accepted and returned.) That loving feeling for his mother's sisters and their husbands always stayed with him.

In the meantime, Martin, who had started his engineering education at the Polytechnic Institute of Brooklyn in February of 1949, was taking driving lessons from Dave's good friend, Sam Berliner.

Martin passed the driving test on his first attempt and was able to drive to the homes of all the relatives who invited them for dinner while Dave and Dottie were out of town. In fact, the boys had an invitation every night of the week to one relative's home or another, but sometimes Martin declined because he had tests for which he must prepare. Martin was all business. Not Paul. He was the social one. He was busy baking cookies to bring to the aunts or grandparents for a dinner gift.

Paul's big day was closing in; his bar mitzvah was scheduled for November 1949, when he would turn thirteen years old.

The literal translation of bar mitzvah is "the Son of the Commandments." The origin of maturity at thirteen years goes far back when maturity was determined solely by the biological yardstick; at puberty, a boy was automatically a man. Despite the fact that he was automatically a bar mitzvah before he was allowed to take his rightful place among his male adult peers, he had to undergo the ritual imposed, which is reading from the Torah before the entire congregation.[77]

Dottie was making all the bar mitzvah arrangements. Because Samson wouldn't drive on Shabbos, they picked the Hebrew Community Center of Boro Park, a few doors from his apartment. Dave and Dottie commissioned Adler Caterers to cater the reception, and they selected the food, flowers, and band. Dottie helped design the unique invitation that looked like the Holy Ark containing the Torah. The front panels were embossed in English and Hebrew and, when opened, revealed the invitation.

The music would be by Bernie Leaf, and the contract included the distribution of a four page book in the shape of a green leaf, including Paul's bar mitzvah picture on the inside front flap. They also distributed a four-page booklet of English and Jewish songs.

No one had ever seen such an unusual invitation and confirmation book before, but Dottie had established herself as being far ahead of her time in everything she did. With the rabbi, she participated in writing the two speeches Paul recited; one after the services and one before the reception. Everything was ready to go.

A week before the bar mitzvah, Dottie told Paul to be careful every time he went out to play in the school yard. She might as well have said it "to the wall." When he played basketball, he played each game as if for the tryouts for the New York Knickerbockers. So one day, Paul went out to play basketball and came back with a black eye. As upset as Dottie was, she was thankful that it wasn't a broken bone. By the next week, most of the blackness had disappeared.

The Friday night before the bar mitzvah, Dottie was filling small sandwich bags with candy to throw when his Torah reading was complete. The throwing of candy is to shower the man with sweetness that he will take with him throughout life.

The religious services took place on Saturday, November 19, 1949. At the end, his father, Dave, recited aloud the ancient formula for severance saying, "Blessed be He who releases me from the responsibility of this child." Since he couldn't read a word of Hebrew, Dave did not know what he was saying.

Oh, if he only had known!

But everything was perfect, from the services, Torah reading, and haftorah, right through the reception. Everyone was happy.

SHORTLY AFTER THE TWO BANKS merged, they received authority to open new offices and, once again, Dave's workload increased dramatically. The bank did not have a registered architect working for it any more. Jack Westney was now a vice president and was in charge of office space. He and Dave would work together for several years. Westney would readily admit that he himself "did not have the hands-on experience with the properties that Dave did. Dave proved to be very effective at his job." Westney went on to say that Dave "had a delightful personality. He was cooperative. He was pleasant. He was decent to deal with. He knew how to coax cooperation out of people into the situations that he had to deal with. He was a very nice man."

Another vice president for the bank, John (Jack) Fischer said that Dave "was a great person and a hard worker who knew his business." These quotations were made fifty years after the fact. Back then, anti-Semitism was still rampant and nasty.

Dave received periodic raises, but they were not commensurate with his talent and the huge profits the bank was making as a result of his efforts. He had to do private work at night to support a better life style. This he called "freelancing," getting jobs on his own, inspecting buildings, drawing up plans, and writing specifications. His problem was the lack of an architectural license required to file plans with the city's building department. He knew all the codes, and he knew all the design criteria as well as any licensed architect or professional engineer, but he did not have the license.

To remedy this problem, Dave entered into an unwritten agreement with his good friend, Morris Brody, a registered architect, who allowed Dave to use the Brody seal and sign his name. Morris received a copy of all the plans Dave signed, plus a stipend. With the money Dave made on freelancing, he was able to pay back all the loans made to him by his friend, Sam Berliner. That eased the stress in the family, but by no means did it eliminate it. Dave still had the rash, still had the maddening itch, and still was angrily disposed toward the young son who was not living up to his standards.

PAUL ENTERED NEW UTRECHT HIGH SCHOOL in 1951, one year before Martin graduated college. Martin then graduated from Officer Candidate School and became an ensign in the navy in 1953. At this time, Mr. Madoff, the owner of 9 Webster Avenue where we lived, sold the house to a man who wanted to have his family occupy the nice apartment rented by the Weinbergs, and attempted to evict them. When Dave and Dottie realized that the courts would sustain the eviction, they started to look for another apartment, and in the spring of 1954 moved to 43-57 Union Street, in Flushing, New York. It was another unusual circumstance for Paul, since he had just started Brooklyn College. His commute to school went from a delightful thirty-minute bus ride to a two-hour train ride in each direction every day. He had to get up very early in the morning to make his physics class that began at eight.

THE GOOD NEWS FOR THE FAMILY was that Dave's rash was now almost completely gone; he was starting to handle the pressure at the bank. The bank president was now calling on Dave to do private work for him that no one else was able to accomplish. The price for the president was also right. The other officers of the bank perceived the warm relationship between Dave and the president and were careful of what they said and did to Dave, at least to his face. They knew that Dave had made it to the ladder and was on the way up.

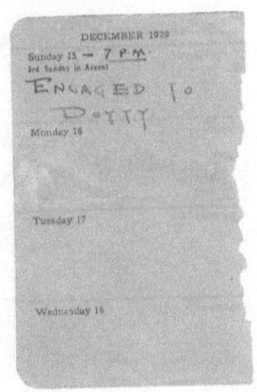

Dave's hand-marked calendar Dec 15, 1929

Dave and Dottie in Alpine (May 1930)

Engagement of Dottie & Dave (April 1930)

Wedding Party of Dottie & Dave (Sept 6, 1930)
Top:Charley Fine, Seymour Schussler, Jules Cohen,
David Weinberg, Mac Weinberg, Harry Liebowitz,
Jack Steg, Sam Steg
Middle: Elsie Marcus, Gussie Saposnick, Frances Weinberg,
Dorothy Weinberg, Mildred Schussler, Lee Saperstein,
Ray Bitterman, Rose Steg
Bottom: Page Boy: Henschel, Flower Girls: Rhoda Pickholz,
Brawerman, Annette Schussler, Yetta (now Etta) Schussler

Building Dept Team at Bank For Savings (6/20/36)
Back: Watkins, Ehresman, Alyea, West, Wack
Middle: Graf, Major, Hodgson, Lambert
Front: Ordwein, Dave Weinberg, Munro, Frank, Picken

Friends at Weinberg residence (Nov 18, 1961)
Back: Irene & George Burch, Sam Berliner, Jack & Terry Keller
Front: Mary Seiden, Jeanne Berliner, Murry Seiden

Dave taking a smoke before a tennis game at
at Rainbow Lodge, Livingston Manor (July 1937)

Dottie with her sons Paul & Martin (July 1937)
at Rainbow Lodge, Livingston Manor (July 1937)

Paul, Dave, Martin (June 1938)

Papa Schussler and Paul, Coney Island (July 1938)

Paul and Dave, Lake Oscawana, N.Y. (July 23, 1939)

Dottie, Dave and Paul (Aug 1940)

Paul & Martin
at 9 Webster Ave, Brooklyn, N.Y. (Sept 1939)

The David Weinberg Family (Feb 1942)
Martin, Dave, Dottie, Paul (on stool)

Dave, Dottie, Paul, Martin (Nov 1, 1945)

Pa, Mac, Irving, Dave

The Pa, Mac, Irving, Dave (circa 1947)

The Ma & The Pa (circa 1930)

Dottie, Dave at Lake Erie (August 1948)

Martin Bar Mitzvah (June 20, 1944)

Paul Bar Mitzvah (November 19, 1949)

Schussler Family (October 14, 1945)
Top: Milton Salant, Sid Kalikow, Dave Weinberg,
Artie Schussler, Sol Pickholz
2nd: Jerome Pickholz, Etta Salant, Mildred Kalikow,
Dottie Weinberg, Sheila Schussler, Mary Pickholz
3rd: Paul Weinberg, Rhoda Pickholz, Charles Schussler,
Samson Schussler, Annette Schussler, Martin Weinberg,
Pearl Kalikow
Bottom: Barbara Kalikow, Adrienne Salant

Ma & Pa 50th anniversary (Sept 15, 1951)
Top: Selma & Marvin Weinberg, Mae W, Paul W, Dave W,
Warren W, Irwin Neveleff, Myron Baum
Middle: Thelma W parents (Harry & Beatrice Geller), Irving W,
Dottie W, Lora Neveleff, Gladys W (Baum), Selma Baum
Pete Peterson
Bottom: Thelma W, Mac W, Fannie W, The Pa (Nathan),
The Ma (Annie), Sam Brawerman, Sarah Goldstein
(Mother of Mae), Frances Peterson, Rachel Peterson

6

Memories and Lessons

I HAVE LOOKED FORWARD to writing this chapter, an important, if not essential part of the book, for it shows the character of my parents, both individually and as a couple. In it, I refer to them as Mom and Dad.

Many friends and relatives have contributed to this chapter. To make this a memory in the truest sense of the word, I have not even made any grammatical changes to their contributions.

Mom and Dad's life changed when they had to move away from their apartment on Webster Avenue in Brooklyn. They had searched for nearly two years to find the cooperative apartment house, commonly called "the co-op," in Flushing, Queens. The name of the complex of three buildings was Franconia Village. The Ashley and Beryck buildings stood between Kissena Boulevard and Union Street. The Cornwall Building was between Union Street and Robinson Street. The entrance to that building faced a private park for the residences' use. Mom and Dad purchased a corner apartment on the second floor, apartment 2H, facing Union Street on one side and the small-grassed area at the rear of the building on the other side. They were one of the first ones to move in, because the courts weren't going to give them any further extensions on the eviction notice served by the new owner of the house in Brooklyn.

Dad was immediately selected as a member of the board of directors. The owners of the co-op were very aware of Dad's knowledge of construction and wanted that type of individual on the board. He served for several years, until the builder was relieved of any further responsibilities.

I had just started my career in Brooklyn College when this move forced me to change addresses and friends. As a result, what should have been a happy occasion, in that we were all starting what seemed to me a new life, was most difficult for me. Mom and Dad's friends could drive to the new apartment without difficulty. My brother, Martin, had gone into the navy and was traveling away from the nest. But I left my neighborhood and my friends and found the new environ-

ment, together with the longer trip to school and the eventual change of schools
to the engineering curriculum at the City College of New York, to be very trying.
As you will see, Mom helped to ease me into the new surroundings.

She did everything she could to make new friends for herself, for Dad, and for
me. As the new apartment dwellers moved into the co-op, she made herself available to help anyone who needed it.

The following is a story contributed by our neighbor, Pauline Block, who
lived in Apartment 2G, right next door. Nostalgically, she said that it was typed
on "the old typewriter the girls used in school, which makes it an antique, but
with enough paper and a bottle of white-out, it served the purpose."[78]

The year was 1955 and 225 eager new couples, mostly with children, were
happily moving into Franconia Village, the spacious new cooperative in
Flushing, Queens. It was one of the first cooperatives to have an all-electric
kitchen, and wonder of wonders, the first to have a dishwasher; an actual
built-in machine.

These refugees from Brooklyn, the Bronx, and wherever, were leaving
smaller cramped quarters, or parents and other relatives with whom they had
been doubling up due to the dire apartment shortage following World War ll.

Franconia had three buildings, and their names had the ring of an English
Village, coming out of the fertile imagination of the builder. They were called
Ashley, Beryck, and Cornwall. Immediately they were called the A, B, and C
buildings.

The Cornwall was also given the name, "the Country Club" by certain
inhabitants of this building, hoping, no doubt, to set themselves apart, and
giving a clue perhaps as to their future aspirations.

Into this superior enclave, the "C Building," moved two families, side by
side. They were the Blocks, Bob and Pauline with one child, Susan, and the
other family, Dottie and Dave Weinberg who had two sons. Martin was in the
navy, and Paul, the younger, was still in school. The families gained their
place on the second floor by becoming known as 2G and 2H respectively.

Dottie and Pauline let each other know how happy they were to have
neighbors like themselves; superior in every way. While Dottie expounded on
her sons' accomplishments, Pauline let Dottie see all the "A" papers of the
girls from school, quickly and quietly tucking away the lesser marks. [Writers
note: Pauline and Bob had a second daughter, Barbara.]

Seriously speaking, the one thing that quickly came out was Dave's accomplishments. Due to his engineering knowledge and building experience, he
was immediately voted onto the board of directors and became one of the
most energetic, hard working and productive members of that body. He
remained on the board for many years, and Franconia was indeed fortunate to

have him, because so much had to be done and so many decisions had to be made.

Being a new board of directors for a new cooperative, which itself was a fairly new concept in apartment house living after the war, was no easy task for this group of novices. They had to tackle the job of dealing with the builder, who only wanted to collect his money and quietly fade away from cooperative complaints, a maze of government regulations, and to boot away everyone who was so-called "Landlord."

Dave was one of the hardest working directors and kept, not only his calm and cool, but also a ready smile for everyone. He was extremely well liked.

Bob not only called on him for advice and expertise, but many tools he lacked. Dave was always ready to help and did so on practically all the additions and improvements we made to our apartment. Bob was a great amateur, and Dave was the expert and overseer.

Equally, I was flanked by two experienced Jewish mothers, Dottie Weinberg and Lena Sobel. How could I not have the best and most practical advice on raising superior children?

Dottie was always available for baby-sitting when an emergency arose, and I tried to reciprocate by providing the extra chairs needed for the dinners and parties she made. I received and forwarded all their mail when they wintered in Florida and Arizona, and they returned the favor in the summer when we went on vacation. I was reminded by my daughter, Barbara, about how thoughtful they were when they went overseas to travel. They asked the various hotel clerks in the places they visited to save all the unusual stamps, which they brought back to her because they knew she collected stamps.

As time went on, Susan became the babysitter for the children of Linda and Paul (who lived across the street), when they went out.

Dottie and Dave kept in touch when they moved to Florida, and when they came to New York and stayed with Linda and Paul, they invited their old second floor neighbors, and we had a wonderful evening just reminiscing.

The last time Bob and I saw them both was when we went to visit Dottie in the hospital where she had gone for tests when they were in New York. Shortly after, we heard Dottie had passed away and Dave returned to Florida.

News filtered back through a neighbor, Sarah Trachtman, who wintered in Florida, that Dave had gotten on with his life and remarried, and we were glad that he had found a soul mate. Mr. and Mrs. Sobel on the other side of me had also passed on, and I say from the bottom of my heart that I never again, living here, had such wonderful neighbors.

I will always think of them both sadly and happily.

Sadly, because time has gone on and events happen over which we have no control. Bob also passed away four years ago (*1993*). Good things pass before we even realize and appreciate them.

Happily, I can think of Dave and Dottie in a time frame when we were younger, healthier, more innocent, and looking to the future with hope for a better life for our children. It was a time when we regarded neighbors as being with our own, and we all shared in one another's "simchas" and "nachas" together.

Now we have the memories, which are warm and wonderful, and as the song says, "they can never take that away."

Since Dad was on the board of directors and was very active with all the owners of the co-op, most of the people in the development knew not only him, but also my mother and me. I had mixed feelings about that situation. Although it was nice to be popular, it was embarrassing for me to walk the neighborhood and be greeted by people I had never met. Not only would they greet me by name, but also they would inquire about my family.

Jewish Holidays [79]

ALTHOUGH WE WERE NOT an orthodox family, we did follow many of the customs of the Jewish faith. The Sabbath, *Shabbos*, which begins at sundown Friday night and ends at sundown Saturday, is considered to be the most holy of all days in the year. It is the day, I was taught, that God rested after creating the world in six days, which made that day holy. Yet, I was allowed to relax on the weekend and was permitted to play ball, ride in the car, write, turn the lights on and off, play with my friends, and do other things that were not permitted by Orthodox Jews. Mom always accepted the honor of ushering in the Sabbath by lighting three Sabbath candles about one half hour before sundown.

The Jewish holidays were different. It was important to Mom that her family respect the holidays and follow most of the traditions.

One of the most dramatic events in the history of the Jews led to the festival of Passover, known as *Pesach,* which is one of the most difficult holidays to observe, due mainly to the dietary laws. In order to appreciate the significance of the holiday, one must understand what precipitated all the laws.

Jacob's favorite son, Joseph, and his seventy family members settled in Egypt. Joseph was second in command to the king of Egypt until a new king made all of them slaves. They suffered severe persecution. Under Moses and Aaron, the Jews pursued their freedom. After speaking with God, Moses warned the king of terrible things that would happen to his people unless he "Let my people go." When the king refused, ten plagues were wrought by God on the Egyptians, the last one being the slaying of the firstborn son.

The twelve loosely organized Hebrew tribes were leaving Egypt, but the angry king wanted to destroy them. The Jews had to flee and did not have the time to bake their bread in the usual way. They also had to leave before the dough had a chance to rise. The dough, baked in the hot sun of the desert, stayed flat and became the first *matzoh*. Moses led his people to the Red Sea and was presumably trapped between the water and the rushing Egyptian Army. However, God parted the sea and allowed the Jews to get to the other side and drowned all the pursuers.

There are several very interesting notes one should make about the holiday of Passover.

This is the first time the twelve tribes were united as a nation, and the Bible considers *Nisan* the first month of the year because this was the month of liberation for the Jews. Therefore, Nisan starts with this holiday and is considered to be the New Year by many Jews. You will read later in the book about *Rosh Hashanah*, which is observed on the first day of the seventh month and considered, by most, to be the Jewish New Year.

The next note to remember is that the Jew felt that no man has a right to make a slave of any man, because all of us were equally created in God's image.

Since the holiday is celebrated with only specially prepared foods, it also is required that for the eight days, we use special dishes, utensils, and linens. The night before Passover begins, the entire family performs a special ceremony of cleansing the house of all *chametz*. Chametz is any mixture of leaven, technically wheat, rye, oats, and barley, that has been mixed with water and allowed to rise. In each room, Mom would place a small piece of bread on a piece of furniture made of wood. Armed with a candle, I would lead my father from room to room searching for the chametz. With a wood spoon in one hand and feather in the other, he would thoroughly clean every last speck from each room into a cloth held by my brother, and tie it tight. The next morning we would take the chametz, feather, and wood spoon all wrapped with a piece of the previous year's *afikomen*, and make a three man crusade to the very dimly lit basement where my brother would toss it all into the coal burning boiler.

A special treat, only at this time of year, was *noent*. I will share the recipe with you:

1 pound of honey
2 pounds of walnuts
2 cups of matzoh farfel-very small pieces of matzoh
3-4 cups of sugar

I was in charge of cracking the walnuts and removing them from the shell and grinding them.

Toast the farfel to golden brown.

Mix the nuts and farfel.

Bring the honey to a boil, and put in mixture of nuts and farfel and cook on medium heat for about fifteen minutes, or until entire mixture is golden brown. Keep stirring with a wooden spoon so that mixture will not burn.

Add sugar and mix thoroughly while cooking for about another five minutes.

Wet board and roll out mixture to desired thickness. *Constantly* keep rolling pin wet so mixture will not stick.

Cut slices and place on wax paper.

I ALWAYS LOOKED FORWARD to *Pesach* for many reasons. Noent was one of them. Mom shared this treat with family and friends. When her brothers were in the army, she would send them noent, along with other goodies they could not get wherever they were stationed.

The first two nights of Passover we had a Seder, usually conducted by one of my grandfathers. My mom's father, Grandpa Sam, who was a very orthodox man, read every word in the *Haggadah* in Hebrew. We didn't start eating for almost two hours. His daughter, Annette, said that Papa was the eldest, and therefore he had the honor of leading the Seder. I remember Mom being proud of me when I, as the youngest male, said the Four Questions, *Fir Kashes*. Grandpa gave me a prominent part in the Seder. After reading the questions, we sang songs like "Dyanu" and "Chad GadYa," and I was told to open and close the door for Elijah, the Prophet who is supposed to precede the coming of the Messiah.

By the time the Seder was over, I was a bit "tipsy" from drinking four cups of wine, the amount described in the *Haggadah*. But I enjoyed nothing more than bargaining with my grandpa for a present, which I would get for returning the afikomen, the hidden matzoh. I hardly remember what I got in the exchange, but I will never forget the fun we had bargaining. Looking back, Grandpa probably had far more fun than I, but my joy is the loving memory of a loving grandpa dialoging with his favorite grandson.

Hag sameach, Happy holiday. *Hag Ha-Matzot*, Happy Feast of Unleavened Bread.

And, of course, *Happy Pesach*, Happy Passover.

IT IS INTERESTING THAT PASSOVER is celebrated thirty days after *Purim*. The reader may wonder why the first of the year is always celebrated thirty days after another holiday. It even happens on a leap year. The Hebrew calendar is adjusted with an extra month. After the month of *Adar*, another month called *Adar Bet* is added. Purim is celebrated on the second Adar. All just coincidental? No. The holidays are calendar coordinated so Purim is always the fourteenth of Adar, and Passover is always the fifteenth of Nisan.

Purim is the first important Jewish holiday of the English calendar, usually celebrated some time between mid-February and mid-March. And what would a Jewish holiday be without a wonderful story?

The story is of Ahashveros, king of Persia, who selected Esther, a cousin and adopted daughter of Mordecai, as his new queen. Shortly thereafter, he appointed as his prime minister, a man named Haman, a mean man who wore a three-cornered hat. Mordecai refused to bow down to him as directed, and Haman persuaded the King to sign a law ordering all Jews in his vast empire to be put to death.

In the meantime, Mordecai discovered a plot of two of the king's guards to assassinate Ahashveros. Mordecai convinced Esther to reveal the plot against King Ahashveros, who was extremely grateful and granted her a wish. She told the king of Haman's plan to kill the Jews and revealed she was Jewish. The king immediately ordered that Haman be executed by hanging.

Mordecai was then appointed prime minister, and he proclaimed this day on which the Jews were saved, as a holiday to be observed every year in remembrance of this miracle. It was said that Mordecai and Esther memorialized the events in a *megilla* (scroll), which is read every year. I remember every time Haman's name was mentioned during Purim services in the synagogue, we would stamp our feet and make noises with a *grogger* (noisemaker).

Mom always made sure that I brought a donation to the Ocean Parkway Jewish Center in Brooklyn. She gave food to her temple.

I enjoyed Purim because Mom would always make *hamantashen*; a three-cornered cake filled with *lekvar*, prune butter, and shaped like Haman's hat. The favorite song of this holiday was called "A Wicked Man." It mentioned Shushan, the town in which Esther lived long ago, and the demise of the wicked man. "Oh today we'll merry, merry be and eat some hamantashen."

Shavuos, a two-day holiday, celebrates the Jewish people receiving the Ten Commandments on Mount Sinai. The story of how the Torah was given to the Israelites through Moses may be found in the Bible (Exodus, Chapter 19–20).

It is said that the Jews became a free people because they accepted the Torah. Although the Israelites were no longer slaves after they had left Egypt, they were still enslaved to many idolatrous ideas until they accepted it. That is one of the main reasons that Passover is so closely tied to Shavuos. It comes fifty days after Passover.

I always wondered why Mom would, uncharacteristically, decorate the kitchen with greenery on this day. Little did I know that this was a reminder of the first fruits of the harvest that were brought to the temple. Many congregations decorate their synagogues with flowers and greenery on this holiday.

I wasn't yet twelve years old on May 14, 1948, but I remember the jubilation of my parents, aunts, uncles, grandparents and neighbors in Boro Park, Brooklyn when Israel was voted statehood by the United Nations. For almost one year, the newly formed state fought off seven Arab countries until an armistice, not a peace agreement, was signed. That ended Israel's War of Liberation.

The Daughters-in-Law Speak

LINDA (BARG) WEINBERG[80] remembers that it was the summer of 1959.

> I had met Paul on a blind date a few weeks prior to our date this Saturday night. We were double dating with my friend Elaine Blatt and Paul's friend Dick Cohen. I don't remember where we intended to go, only that there was an airplane event—maybe a crash—at Idlewild Airport (now JFK Airport in Queens), and all the traffic in the area was being diverted. As we couldn't get to our destination, and we were close to the Van Wyck Expressway, Paul suggested that we go to his apartment (actually his parents' apartment). We drove to Flushing, parked the car in front of the building at 43-57 Union Street and took the elevator up one floor. We entered apartment 2H. It was a beautifully furnished apartment, tastefully decorated with many lovely items. I was impressed. The Weinbergs were out for the evening, so we sat in the living room and talked.
>
> Shortly after we arrived, Paul's parents returned and were surprised to find the four of us there. They were very friendly, warm and hospitable. Paul's mother immediately said she was going to make coffee for us and went into the kitchen. In a few minutes we heard a grinding noise, and the aroma of freshly ground coffee beans wafted into the living room. My father had a coffee grinder in his grocery store, but nobody I knew ground coffee beans at home. I was to learn that my mother-in-law was always ahead of her time. The coffee was set to perk on the stove, and Paul's mother set the table.
>
> She called us into the kitchen where they had a nook (something else I had never seen in anyone's home) and a beautifully set table. Each place was set with a bone china cup, saucer and cake plate, all different patterns, but all absolutely beautiful. In the center of the table was a bone china cake plate with attached sugar and creamer. It was the loveliest table setting I had ever seen.

Paul's parents were delightful hosts and made me, Elaine, and Dick feel very welcome.

Little did I know that I would become their daughter-in-law. After Paul and I married, every now and then his parents would present us with a bone china cup, saucer and cake plate, in different patterns, of course. As we both loved them, we too began to purchase them. To this day, on special occasions, we serve coffee and cake on our special china. It always reminds me of my first meeting with the Weinbergs.

My mother-in-law had beautiful taste in furnishing and had many lovely pieces of furniture, antiques, and bric-a-brac. One item that I was particularly taken with was a small teapot with an unusual shape. After my in-laws passed away, I always wondered what had happened to it. You can imagine my delight when looking through a carton of their belongings that had been stored in our attic, we found the teapot. It is proudly displayed in our home and, of course, always reminds me of my mother-in-law. My in-laws were always very kind to me and respectful of me as I was of them.

Myrna Barg, Linda's mother writes[81] that she and her husband, Nat, met Dorothy and Dave when Linda became engaged and "found them to be very devoted parents and, eventually, grandparents." They were always "very fond of Linda as she was of them. They were good hosts and we enjoyed visiting with them. Dorothy and Dave will be missed by all" who knew them.

The first daughter-in-law had some similar memories and some that were diametrically opposite. My brother, Marty, dated a girl by the name of Elaine Schwartz whom he had met in Fire Island.[82]

We dated a couple of times and he decided to bring me home to meet his parents before going to Motel on the Mountain for dinner. Your mother was expecting me and yet she was dressed in a housedress and curlers. Marty told her he was going to bring this girl that he met on Fire Island without giving any explicit details of her. So she expected a Fire Island Hippie. What she got was me. It was a Sunday afternoon, and I don't remember anything except the housedress and curlers. The apartment was clean and it was decorated. It was very nice.

Marty and I decided to get married three weeks and five dates after meeting. We started looking for rings and going back and forth to jewelers, getting stones, and going to the apartment and sharing them with Marty's parents, who I found to be nice, warm, and *hamisha* people. My future mother-in-law said to me: "If you think that this guy is Prince Charming, you got another guess coming. He's no prince." I was pre-warned.

Marty's father was a quiet gentleman. His mother had a set of cups and saucers that I admired, and as a result, she started us on a collection, which I seriously embellished.

As for decorating, I would always stick my two cents in where that was concerned. She eventually took my advice and decorated with suggestions that I gave her.

The Grandchildren Have Their Chance

MONA WAS THE ELDER DAUGHTER of my older brother Martin and Elaine and was Mom and Dad's first grandchild. Most of Mona's recollections[83] of her grandma and grandpa were the days when she traveled to Flushing, New York to visit with them.

Every time we went there, I felt like I was going to a party. The smells of Grandma's soup and noodles permeated the hall from the time we arrived on the second floor.

Grandma always had different games for us to play. As a matter of fact, everything she did with us was a game. It was a carnival atmosphere. It was always special. Cooking was a game. She would let me help pour the ingredients for the soup into the pot and stir. Cleaning was a game. She would tell me where all the soot on the windowsills came from and "allowed" me to help remove it. She was so smart.

One of the strongest memories is of the "one-on-one" talks that we had. If we were in the house we might have talked about my dad when he was a youngster and getting cream cheese all over him, or the unique language that he had all to himself. If we were out walking she might have told me about the volunteer work she did with the Children's Asthmatic Foundation, helping with the ongoing work of her allergist, Doctor Peshkin. Sometimes she would go into detail about grandpa and how he first started out in the field of architecture. She would tell me how difficult it was to be accepted by his peers and bosses because he was Jewish. She would talk about friends, family and neighbors. There wasn't anything she would not discuss. That is why we were so close.

The best part is that she never wanted us to leave. She would follow us to the elevator, and as the inside door was about to close to allow us to travel down to the lobby, she would open the door and start the process over again.

Grandma and Grandpa made a surprise tenth anniversary party for my parents and you (Paul) and Linda. I danced with my sister and my cousins and with Grandma and Dad. It was so memorable that I wanted to make a special party for my parents a few years later and pay for it with money that I had saved. I asked Grandma to help because I didn't know how to plan it or coordinate it, and she was my right hand. She made me feel like a million dollars.

She went shopping with me to the local appetizing store, Sheppy's, and ordered the hors d'oeuvres and all the other food. She ended up paying for the majority of it, but she loved making parties and making people happy. It indicated the type of person she was. It is a memory I will always have. By the way, the party was a great success.

My relationship with Grandpa improved after Grandma passed away because it was only him on whom I was focusing. Before that, I would spend most of my time with her. After that, Grandpa wanted to be involved with everything. He was anxious to hear everything that was going on in my life, especially after we moved to Florida. He wanted us to visit and come with the kids. He wanted to know how everybody was doing. When he was sick, he would still want to know about everybody else in the family. With or without his new wife, Mim, he would love to be part of our family.

Grandma and Grandpa were very fond of their family. Grandma in particular. Grandpa was harder to get to know. He had a harder outside, but he had a very large inside, kind, giving and thoughtful. Many people didn't get a deep involvement with him, and he got over-shined a little bit. Grandma was more open and was able to bring in more people because she was more sociable and outgoing. But if you really got to know Grandpa, he was equally giving and really had everybody's interest at stake. He wanted to help everybody as much as he could. He had harder things to handle, like Mim. That was a difficult part of his life.

STACY WAS PAUL AND LINDA'S elder daughter and Mom and Dad's second grandchild. Mom had a special attachment to Stacy, and the feeling was very much mutual. "Grandma made me feel special, but I never felt that Grandma treated me any more special then the other three." Stacy remembers[84] a loving relationship she had with her grandma, doing various things with her.

I remember making beaded flowers and fruits. There was a fake, fuzzy apple into which we stuck beaded pins. After covering the entire apple with the red beads, we got this shiny beaded apple.

I remember going with Grandma Dottie to get her hair cut or hair done. It might have been just me, and I remember the manicurist putting clear nail polish on my nails. I was young, in the single digits, and I was made to feel special. That was Grandma Dottie. She always made me feel special.

Grandma and Grandpa were always good to us, but we had to behave to their standards. Elyce and I slept at their apartment one night, and they had bought us each a Spirograph. We came home to their apartment and started jumping on the bed. Grandma and Grandpa got mad at us and wouldn't let us play with the Spirograph sets. They took them away and said we couldn't play with them. But they softened and gave them back to us. We still have them.

Then there were the walks that we took with Grandpa. We would walk between the building of the co-op and run ahead of Grandpa, like kids do. He was always slow behind us, and we lovingly called him the Weakly Duckling. I don't know where it came from, but he was always the Weakly Duckling. Sometimes we would walk to get the newspaper at a candy store. That store always had a distinctive smell. I remember the smell of the big cardboard boxes that contained ice cream Creamsicles.

Then there was the "Drawer." Grandpa had a drawer in the bedroom where he kept gum, Dentyne, and maybe mints and Hershey's Special Dark Chocolate. It was the big bar broken up into squares. It felt wonderful being allowed to go into their bedroom and look through their stash of goodies. It was a treat. Everything at Grandma and Grandpa's house was a treat.

I remember eating dinner there and Grandma making brisket. It was a big family and she used to make chicken soup and noodles. Mona and I used to sit with our backs against the wall with the mural wallpaper, which was pink and green. After eating Grandma's soup we got very hot and so was born the name "hot seat."

After Grandma died, Grandpa became a lot more resourceful in the kitchen. He also felt that whatever we wanted to do was good with him. Elyce and I were still kids, but if we wanted to go swimming, he'd say, "use my sun screen, take these towels, and here's the key to the apartment." Then he showed us where to go and what to do and just said to go and have fun.

I felt that Grandma and Grandpa treated all of their grandchildren in a very loving way. They took us to different places, like the Botanic Gardens in Queens. They made all of us feel very special and we were very lucky to have grandparents like them.

ELYCE IS PAUL AND LINDA'S second daughter and Mom and Dad's third grandchild. She writes:[85]

My memories of Grandma Dottie and Grandpa Dave are warm and wonderful. I distinctly remember Grandma Dottie's name for me was "Precious." I don't know if she called any or all of the other granddaughters that, but whenever she called me "Precious," she made me feel like it was only me. She cupped my chin in her hand as she pulled me close and looked into my eyes always with a smile and a twinkle in her eye, and I knew that she really meant it. I loved her. She wore an apron tied around her neck and waist, always in her proper shoes with her glasses on a chain around her neck. She always cut up fruit on the kitchen counter and whenever we came into the house she would summon us into the kitchen and pop something in our mouth. I remember fresh orange slices mostly. Her apartment was the first time I ever saw the "Honey Bear." We used honey on everything; *challah*, fruit ... and I recall the sweetness of those days in that apartment. I was just standing in my kitchen cutting up apples for my kids. I poured honey from the "Honey Bear" and brought it to Jacob and Molly and they gobbled up the sweet fruit. I couldn't help but be reminded of Grandma Dottie. To this day, I get warm and cozy feelings thinking of Grandma each time I eat honey. It was surely a staple in her home as I have made it in mine.

Grandma was proper and poised, as so many people remember her. I, too, remember her like that but along with it was a loving side that was so warm. She was never too proper to bend down and give her granddaughters big hugs. I remember them as frequent and squishy. I don't think she ever wanted to let go. But part of that proper side of her loved the graceful side of life. I always remember her being so fond of dancers and the graceful stance they always held; the way they held their hands and placed their feet with pointed toes. To this day, whenever I see a dancer in a graceful pose, especially my own daughter, I think of how Grandma Dottie would have loved that.

Everything was orderly, and there were beautiful and untouchable things around, but the room had such a deliberate beauty, containing things they had accumulated over the years and also from their many exotic trips. But there was always stuff for us to play in the second bedroom; a carriage filled with dolls and toys. I remember an organ, too. And that big, wonderful color TV. I remember watching all the special TV shows; the Wonderful World of Disney and holiday specials when we went to Grandma and Grandpa's apartment for dinner.

Grandma always had soup. I loved her split pea soup with barley. Grandpa always had a little dish of salt *(a saltcellar)*. He took salt with his fingers and sprinkled a little into his food: salad, soup, everything. I remember flanken. I hated it, but it was such a staple in their home. I don't remember if it was my dad or Grandpa who told the story of why he wouldn't eat chicken. (He saw one being slaughtered, I think.) I also remember that he didn't like pizza, something I could never fathom; pizza lover that I was/am.

I have a memory of Grandpa taking us, the four granddaughters, to the Botanical Gardens. The four girls ran ahead of Grandpa, and as he walked behind us, we would giggle and call him "The Weakly Duckling." We laughed and teased him, all in good fun. I'm sure he enjoyed it too. I always knew that the four of us, all of the granddaughters, were so special to Grandma and Grandpa. They treated us like little princesses, and that is how I always felt around them.

Another one of my memories about their apartment is the "gum drawer." In their bedroom, in the polished wood dresser, was a drawer just filled with gum; Dentyne, packs of hockey cards, football cards, all containing gum. It was always such a special treat to get something out of the "gum drawer." I remember being very excited to get a piece, but then when I put it in my mouth-YUCK. It was always hard and old. God knows how long they had that stuff in there, but even so, I would always ask again, and it would always be a special treat to get it. Grandma used to keep these huge bars of Hershey's Special Dark chocolate in the hall closet and would break off small pieces for

Stacy and me. I think that's where my love for that candy developed, and I still love it to this day.

Another treat was going on the bus into town with Grandma. The bus was very exciting but a little scary. We wouldn't always get a seat together. It was like an adventure ride. You had to hold on as the bus swayed. I loved to pull the bell cord to get off. Sometimes we would walk to Kissena Boulevard with Grandma with her shopping cart to get groceries. There was a grocer named Normy who had a fruit stand, and he used to give us gum. We loved our gum! He was always nice to Grandma and us.

I remember Grandma Dottie with such deep love. She was warm and thoughtful, caring and nurturing. She always made me feel special and loved. I remember Grandpa Dave with great big smiles and always happy to see us. He had such pride in his family. He had a great sense of humor, sometimes "corny," but always fun to be with. I miss them both, but they live in my father. My father has the best of both of them. Grandpa's sense of order: I remember going through Grandpa's closet after he died and we just laughed and laughed when we found fifty years of proofs of purchases. When my dad had his desk in the office downstairs in our house in Merrick, and I might have asked for a red magic marker or a pair of scissors, he would give me exact directions; "in the second drawer on the left side behind the carbon paper and under the glue." Lo and behold, it would always be right where he said it was. I don't doubt that he got that from Grandpa Dave. I see that every day in my dad. I see it when he is with us and especially when he is with his beloved grandchildren. When I see him with them, I can't help be reminded of the wonderful memories I have with my grandparents. I thank God that my children will grow up with fond and loving memories of their beloved grandparents as well. Thank you for giving them and me wonderful memories and letting me share mine with you, Dad. I love you, Elyce.

SHERYL IS MARTIN AND ELAINE'S younger daughter and Mom and Dad's youngest and last grandchild. She remembers[86] her arrival, by elevator, on the first floor of the co-op in Flushing and the walk down the corridor to the last door on the right.

Grandma would always be there, apron on, door open, waiting to greet us. The scent of soup or the aroma of something cooking in the kitchen greeted our noses.

While waiting for dinner, Stacy, Mona, Elyce, and I would retire to the TV room in the back of the apartment. We did not have any toys with which to play, so we would produce skits. After dinner, we would perform for the family, to everyone's delight. I remember that Grandpa's spare change was our reward for our wonderful shows. If we came home with pennies in our pockets, we were rich.

Oh, Grandpa's "sock drawer." That is what I called the drawer where Grandpa's socks were neatly stacked on the right side and more bubble gum than I had ever seen was strewn on the left side. After the quiet time after dinner, the four girls would head toward the bathroom.

Grandpa and Grandma had their bedroom just to the right of the bathroom, and we sauntered into the bedroom to take our gum and run. I don't know if the gum was fresh or stale. What I do remember was the great taste of the sugar going down my throat and making cavities in my teeth.

Two things I remember of Grandma. She was a terrific cook. She gave us the food we wanted. I liked spaghetti with ketchup. Grandpa never ate spaghetti because he said it looked like worms, so Grandma never made tomato sauce. I loved her spaghetti and ketchup. I loved it so much that I requested that dish when I went on my very fancy honeymoon on the luxury Italian Cruise Ship.

The other thing I remember about Grandma Dottie was her beadwork and the patience she had teaching "her girls." She would often sit down with us and try to teach us. After making a few flowers, she would fine tune it with some twists and twirls. I don't remember if I ever walked out of her apartment with my flowers, but to this day, I have flowers made by my Grandma Dottie sitting in my living room.

Grandpa Dave was always tinkering with tools fixing a variety of things. One of his favorite things to fix, other than the things I broke, was clocks. He seemed to have a fascination with them and always fixing them in his hobby area. When I married, Grandpa gave us money, which we used to buy a grandfather clock, which now stands in my living room, engraved with the words "Love Grandpa Dave." That was done while he was alive, and it meant a lot to him.

I was a bit older when they moved to Miami, Florida. I remember that Grandpa did not lose the habit of putting olive oil in his hair to keep his hair young and to preserve its color. He also did not lose the habit of putting a dash of salt in his food. He had a small dish that would only fit two fingers of his hand to pick a pinch of salt and add it to his dishes, whether it needed it or not.

Grandma Dottie had her own home remedies. She made a disgusting concoction for my sore throat. It consisted of tea, orange juice, and a huge amount of honey. More honey than anything else. She said to drink it up; you'll feel better. I don't know if it worked, but the next day I was running around, sans sore throat. I did find it interesting that after I married and had my own children that a doctor told me to use that very same mixture for my children, as an instant remedy for sore throats.

One of the lessons I learned from Grandpa Dave is there is always a solution to a problem. Whether the problem be a broken item that had multiple pieces to puzzle together or if it was a disagreement in principle, there was always a solution. One just had to work with determination to find the right pieces to complete the puzzle.

Number One Son Tells His Story

MARTIN, MOM AND DAD'S first son remembers[87] Dad's teaching him the "facts of life."

I guess I was between ten and fifteen years old at the time. He gave me a little booklet and told me to read it and ask any questions. I read it and told him I have no questions.

I did not do too much shopping for Mom. Maybe I went to buy bread or soup greens or butter from the stores on Eighteenth Avenue. The grocer sold butter by the tub. They would cut out a hunk of butter and weigh it. Mom never took me shopping and never taught me how to shop.

It was a family desire that the boys play an instrument. I remember taking accordion lessons for six months, just after getting into high school in 1945. Then I stopped. I became as expert as I could. I learned the keys, I learned the buttons, I learned the songs and I learned rhythm. I think the reason that I took accordion lessons was because the accordion was being rented, and for the one rental cost both kids were able to practice the same instrument. It was cost effective.

I graduated the Ocean Parkway Jewish Center. My first Hebrew lessons were with Rabbi Leff. He had a place on Eighteenth Avenue across from P.S. 192 (between Forty-seventh and Forty-eighth Streets). He had a one-room classroom, and it was in his classroom that I learned to detest Hebrew school. He carried a stick in his hand. We learned words, how to read and write. I hated it and it was the only time in my life that I played Hooky (stayed out of school). There were some private houses on Eighteenth Avenue, and I hid behind the garbage cans in front of those houses for two hours before going home. I never told Mom.

I remember the Seders we had. There was an army of people. It was very *fraluch* (happy). "Chad Gad Ya" was always sung. Annette, Rhoda and I were always drunk and very giddy by the end of the night. I don't remember bargaining for the afikoman, but I do remember cleaning the house of chametz. One of us held the candle and one the napkin. Dad brushed the bread from the wood furniture. I looked forward to taking it down to the boiler.

I remember Mom putting the laundry out on the clothesline from the kitchen window on the side of the house. I also washed the outside of the windows. We lived on the second floor, and I sat on the windowsill to do it.

Those are the recollections of my childhood with Mom and Dad.

Mom's Siblings Chat

MILLIE REMEMBERS[88] THAT Dave was the strict one, not only with me and Marty, but with our mother, too.

His word was law, and he ruled with an iron hand. Dottie was the easygoing kind. Like all the Schussler girls, she was spotless in her home, and we all kept our children (your generation) spotless, too. Not one child went in for sports as you (Paul) did, but then, which one of your uncles played ball or took you to a ball game? Uncle Sid! There is no doubt that your parents loved both of you equally. However, Marty was the serious and studious one, while you were the *bren* (quick and with fire) with personality plus! Marty and you were dressed alike. You were a slob. But when you walked out of the house, you were a nice little boy. Marty also. Marty was a clean boy.

"Dottie was a typical older sister to me, always looking out for my interests," said Artie[89], who was born in 1916, eight years after Dottie.

> When I was in the army during World War II, she kept in constant touch with me by mail or packages of food, like "noent" and the like. She was very talented in the arts. When she was younger she would play the piano, and to this day I remember her playing one of my favorite pieces called "The Doine." She was also talented in needlework."
>
> Dottie and Dave visited us in Detroit every year and watched our children grow up. They always joined us in our many simchas, happy occasions. Sometimes we would reminisce about the foods our mother made. One was a *pletzlach*. Dottie gave me the ingredients and proceeded to demonstrate how to make it into a real delicacy. Sometime later, we decided to make it together. I was given the task of squeezing the potato mixture in the cheesecloth, but I didn't know my own strength. We all had a good laugh when the mixture ended up on the kitchen ceiling. So much for my pletzlach career.

Etta[90] and Annette[91] both said how helpful Dad was to them in their times of need. Annette was not the only one to say that Mom was born before her time.

> She was the first person that I can remember who wore rings on all her fingers. She was the first to put beads on the kitchen window as curtains. I copied that idea for my bathroom window. She was very artistic. She made the most beautiful beaded flowers. She also knitted lovely sweaters and outfits. When the Family Circle met in her house, everyone at the table had their own saltshaker. Each person at the table had a different colored cup and saucer. She started having games at the family gatherings. Mary was the president, and Mom was the secretary.

"Dottie was a loveable person. She always got along with everyone. I will put Dave in the same category. Very helpful to me." These were quotes from Charles.[92] He continued, "both were always interested in my well-being.

Whether it was at my bar mitzvah, where I performed as a cantor, or how I did in school, sung at concerts or going overseas to war, they were always there. When I was preparing to go overseas, I gave Dave secret words so he would be able to decipher my letters when I was in North Africa and Italy (combat zones)." Charles concluded that, "these two were wonderful people to know."

From the writer's memory, Mom was proud of her young brother who had become an accomplished singer by the age of nine.

Honesty and Character

IT WAS THE SPRING OF 1950, and I was just past my thirteenth birthday and going to the Boy Scout Meeting at Public School 48 on Eighteenth Avenue and Sixtieth Street in Brooklyn as I did every Friday night. We would line up in groups and have our meetings in which we would learn about a scout being loyal, trustworthy, friendly, courteous, kind and obedient. These were traits that were taught by my parents and reinforced by the Scout Law. After the first part of the meeting, the troop would break up into groups. Some were given lessons in a variety of merit badges, and some were given lessons on graduating to the next level after Tenderfoot, the entering level of a Scout. These lessons were given in different classrooms.

One night, I saw a foreign coin on a teacher's desk, and I thought it would be nice if I had it. When no one was looking, I put the coin in my pocket where it rested until I arrived home. The next day I showed the coin to Mom, telling her that I had found it. Mom had this uncanny knack of seeing right through me. She knew I didn't *find* it.

"What a beautiful coin. Where did you find it," she asked?

"At the Boy Scout meeting."

"That's wonderful, and where did you find it?" she persisted.

"Oh, in a classroom."

Notice, I never lied to Mom. I just answered her questions.

Looking me right in the eye, she knowingly continued, "How lucky, and where in the classroom did you find it?"

Continuing my honest answers, I admitted, "On the teacher's desk."

Lovingly, Mom said, "That's stealing and that's not right. That coin is not yours. You did not find it. It belongs to someone else. On Monday morning that teacher will be missing her coin and not feeling too happy. How would you feel if someone took something that you loved and enjoyed? What do you think you should do?"

I couldn't wait until the next meeting the following Friday night to run up to the same room and deposit the coin in the exact same spot as I took it.

It was a lesson in honesty and integrity that still lives within me. Thanks, Mom.

In her very subtle ways, Mom knew where I was and what I was doing all the time. She was eager to love me and quick to teach me right from wrong. She would ask where I was, with whom I played, what I played, and other questions showing a loving interest in me. "You are judged by the company you keep," she would always preach. "Maintain friendships with nice people."

One particular day when I was eleven years old, she asked why it took me so long to bring home a small order from the vegetable store, which was around the corner and across Eighteenth Avenue.

I explained that a middle aged woman had just finished her order and was loaded with four paper bags; two heavy ones and two light ones. The storekeeper asked if I would help her home with her shopping, and said I would be tipped handsomely, since she lived five blocks away and gave good tips.

I accepted, and he handed me the two largest and heaviest bags. There were no plastic bags with handles in 1947. Everything was packed in paper

My arms were aching after walking only a block, but I continued. I remembered that I could not stop, for I gave my word that I would deliver. In the back of my mind I felt that I would be getting more than the usual ten-cent tip.

To answer Mom's question, I told her of my experience delivering the order. After the five-block walk, she asked that I carry the order up the front steps and then up the flights of stairs to her apartment. I held back the tears from the pain in my arms. I continued to hold the packages while she fished for her keys and opened the door and told me to deposit the packages on the kitchen table. There upon, she placed three coins in my hand. Unbelievably, I looked at the three pennies. Returning them to her, I politely said that she needed it more than I.

Mom was quick in her praise, saying that I was kind to help someone in distress, and that I was a gentleman, but that the woman who gave me the ungracious tip was no lady. I never took another delivery job from the vegetable man again.

Not all lessons came quickly to me. The term "tough love" was not yet a coined expression, but Mom knew how to handle her "boy." I was not what one considered a neat kid. I was neat and clean for school, and that was it. After school, I changed my clothes, and off I ran to the schoolyard, leaving my pants, shirt, and tie lying on the bed, with one shoe at the head of the bed and the other shoe at the end. It took a while to train me to hang my things in the closet. However, the most difficult job for Mom was to get me to put my house slippers in the closet before I went to school. One day she told me that my slippers might disappear if they were not put away. I made a sign that read, PUT SHOES AWAY, but that did not help.

One day when I returned home from school, I couldn't find my slippers. Mom said they must have disappeared. Perhaps they flew out the window, and I should look outside in the fenced side yard. Sure enough, they were there. I had to retrieve them by going to the landlord, Mr. Madoff, and getting a key to the cellar. He did not like me, and I did not like him. He didn't even like it when I played stoopball on the concrete steps in front of the house. That story, later. To me he was a mean man.

It was not a pleasant trip. I unlocked the wood door to the cellar. Reaching high on my toes, I flipped on the light switch on the left inside wall to barely light the dark dungeon cellar. As I opened the creaking door to the cellar it revealed a wobbly wooden staircase that led downstairs to the boiler on the left side, coal piled high and the open storage space on the right. The tenants never worried about theft. To reach the hatch door to the rear yard, I had to walk past the boiler and pull the light cord on the porcelain fixture that barely illuminated the rear part of the cellar. As scary as that was, the physical part was pushing the heavy wooden hatch to the open position. After retrieving my slippers, I had to reverse the process.

Mom said I would find them there every day they were not put away. Guess what? I never left my slippers, or for that matter, any of my shoes, lying around again. Once again, a lesson that has never left me. I am extremely neat and organized in everything I do.

MY COUSIN JEROME PICKHOLZ relates the following:[93]

> When you asked me to think of something special about my Aunt Dottie, the first thing that came to mind was her unique way of signing autograph albums. I'm talking about the albums we had signed by friends and relatives when graduating from elementary and junior high schools. Many of the pages started with "Roses are red, violets ...," you know the rest. But not my Aunt Dottie's page. You could always depend on her to write "CHARACTER COUNTS." and write it in a most distinctive way. [Writers note: Alone on a line with dots surrounding the words CHARACTER COUNTS] I saw the phrase first when she signed my sister Rhoda's album when I was seven or eight years old. I had no idea what the phrase meant but I was certain that I would when I reached the sixth grade. No such luck.

When the big day arrived, and she signed my album, I was still in the dark, still didn't know what it meant. It seemed very erudite, profound, and I was proud to have it in my album. Some think like a rite of passage, and I had obviously earned the right to have a page with that entry in my very own album. By the ninth grade, I had learned a little algebra, Latin, American History, civics, music, art, graduated with honors, Arista, and all. And I had Aunt Dotties' page prominent in my album. But I still didn't know exactly what it meant.

I'm now a grandfather. I've traveled the world; been there! Done it! But if you want to know what "CHARACTER COUNTS" really means, don't ask me.

Oh, I now know the full and inner meaning. But it's a secret. A secret between my Aunt Dottie and me.

Stories From The Past

I LEARNED TO BE CREATIVE and frugal by watching Dad. My allowance was so small; I not only couldn't, but also wasn't allowed to, purchase toys on my own. A nickel's worth of marbles was out of the question. I never purchased a penny pack of bubble gum which came with baseball cards, which we called "tickets." These are things for which I had to compete and win. I would never want to come home and tell my Mom that I lost marbles or "tickets." I became a very competitive person.

Mom would send me to the grocery store, sometimes called the "dairy store" for canned goods or dairy products. There I would purchase bottles of milk—no containers back then—butter, cream cheese, which, like the butter, would be cut from a slab that was approximately four inches by four inches and twelve inches long. The cheese would be stored in a foil wrap, which would be shipped to the "dairy" in a wooden box. Sometimes I would get lucky and the "dairy" owner would give me the box. I would remove the top and cut three unequal size holes in the long side of the box. I could do this because Dad had a nice collection of tools, nails, and screws. If I wasn't able to cut, drill, or saw, Dad was always there to help. I was now ready to play a marble game with my friends.

I gave them no easy task, since I wanted to win. They would stand halfway across the street and roll a marble, called the "shooter," toward the box. If their "shooter" entered the largest hole in the middle, they would get their marble back, plus three more. If their "shooter" entered one of the smaller side holes, they would get their marble back, plus five. In the very unlikely event of the "shooter" entering the smallest hole, which just fit the marble, they would get their marble plus ten. With a thirst for increasing their collections, the kids lined up to be suckered out of their marbles. There was no such thing as "Atlantic City

Gambling" back then, but this form of roulette earned me a large collection of what we called "immees."

THERE WAS NO SUCH THING as a supermarket back then, either. Around the block, across Eighteenth Avenue, was a candy store on the corner where Dad got his cigarettes, then the kosher butcher, the fish market, the grocery, the bakery, the vegetable store, another store, the barber, and finally the hardware store. Sometimes Dad would send me to the candy store to buy Camel Cigarettes that would cost nineteen cents a pack, unless I bought a carton, and then the price would drop to fifteen cents a pack. There were times that I would watch the butcher clean a chicken and watch the fish man clean, scale, and gut a fish. The bakery would smell so good. We would buy our fresh corn bread, rye bread, or pumpernickel, as well as cakes, cookies and Charlotte Russes. Yum! A Charlotte Russe was a small piece of cake covered with lots of whipped cream and topped with a cherry, all wrapped in a circular piece of cardboard.

When I went shopping with Mom to help carry the packages, she would show me how to select good fruit and vegetables. Little did I know how handy that training would be in the future. The storeowners liked my mother. She was always a perfect lady. No one ever called my mother "honey" or "sweetie." The owners always picked the best produce for Mom, and they showed me how they did it. Mom always felt it was important for the family to eat only the best foods.

The *noshes*—snacks—had to be healthy. When I entered my teens, I developed a case of acne. When I went to college, I kept very late hours. I would sometimes be studying into the early morning. Mom knew that I would want to nosh, so instead of filling up a bowl of sweets that were bad for the complexion, she filled a Tupperware breadbasket, kept in the refrigerator, with cut up carrots, celery, green pepper, and cucumber, which to this day are my favorite snacks.

UNTIL THE LANDLORD BOUGHT a new refrigerator and gave us his old one, we had what was called an "ice box." We purchased big chunks of ice from an ice vendor who drove through Webster Avenue yelling, "ICE, ICE, ICE FOR SALE!" He would cut a chunk to fit the particular icebox, put a waterproof cloth on his shoulder, pick up the chunk with large pointed tongs and carry it on his shoulder to the apartment.

ALMOST EVERY SUNDAY EVENING found us at a restaurant with the Kalikows, Mom's sister, her husband, Sid, and their children, Penny and Barbara. We would usually dine at the dairy restaurant on Thirteenth Avenue, called "The

Famous," or go for deli on Twelfth Avenue. My favorite foods were dairy products, and that earned me the nickname, "*Milichdica Yink*"—Dairy Boy. Another nickname I inherited was "*Langa Luch*," meaning long noodle, because I was tall and skinny. Both names were used lovingly, and I loved it. I would usually be starved when we got to the restaurant and would order more than I ever ate. It got to a point where Dad would tell me that my "eyes were bigger than my stomach."

The Kalikows and the Weinbergs always had a good time together.

MOM AND DAD FELT that it was important to send their boys to sleep-away camp. It was an important part of growing up, cutting the umbilical cord, and putting and keeping us in a rather close environment over an extended period without the shoulders of Mommy and Daddy.

Camp Olympus was the first camp I attended. I started at the age of four and a half, and my brother Martin was ten. The owners of the camp were the Kasins, always called "Mom and Pop Kasin." They were warm and wonderful people and were the reason for the camp's success. I went to "sleep-aways" until I reached the age of seventeen.

In all those years, Dad always packed the trunk and duffle bag in such an organized way that he was able to fit more things than anyone ever thought. I would watch him so that I would be able to pack for the return trip home. Of course, on visiting day, they would help by taking some of the things I would not be using during the second four weeks of camp.

Receiving packages from home was the most exciting fun. The bigger the package, the more kids who gathered around to see what there was to share. I always had the biggest goodie "cubby." My parents would send up an eight-pack of Campfire Marshmallows, which I would share with my bunkmates at the next bonfire. We would shave a long, skinny stick to a point onto which we impaled a marshmallow. Then we'd hold it at arm's length over the flame until it was lightly tanned or caught fire and was crisply toasted. Either way, they tasted delicious. When I was older, our parents would include salami, which I shared with everyone.

Mom and Dad were into "stretching" a happy event. Mom had a saying: "Make parties. Life is so short; take advantage of the happy occasions. Make parties." She wanted happiness to pervade our lives, so she might tell me an exciting upcoming event but leave out a detail or two, so I could get double the pleasure.

Our next-door neighbors on Webster Avenue, Pauline and Sam Schmier, had two daughters, Florence and Rhoda. Rhoda was one year my junior, and we used to spend time together. She was my unannounced girl friend. Those days, boys did not have girl friends, or at least did not tell anyone of their propensity for girls. It was sissy-ish to have a girl friend.

The Schmiers had something the Weinbergs did not, and that was a television. They had a seven-inch black-and-white set for which they eventually purchased a magnifier so they and their guests could watch Uncle Milty. Sometimes I got to see the wrestler Antonino Rocco do his famous flying drop kicks on the "bad guys."

It was the summer of 1952, and I was at Camp Watitoh when my parents came up and told me they had bought a television set. I was very excited because they told me it was slightly larger than the Schmier's set. After camp, I came home expecting to see a ten or twelve inch screen. Was I surprised when I walked into the living room to see a sixteen-inch set! That was just like my parents. They would give you some good news, but save part of it so there would be two nice feelings from one happy event.

MOM AND DAD ALWAYS involved themselves, sometimes to a fault, in the lives of their boys. When we graduated Officer Candidate School in Newport, Rhode Island, Mom and Dad attended our graduations. Taking trips to visit and be with their children was part of their life. When Martin was in Camp Lejune, North Carolina, serving his country in the navy, they visited him. When Paul was stationed in Pensacola Florida, his billet was the staff of the Chief of Naval Air Training. They drove from New York to visit him and to meet his fellow officers and civilian staff who worked for him. They stayed at a nearby motel but spent every day together with him. Love of family was the underlying reason for taking the trips.

Dad wasn't making enough money for all the "necessary extras" in our family life, so he worked nights on his private jobs. He would sit at his drafting table and draw up plans and write specifications for the rehabilitation of private residences. Martin and I somehow knew that Mom and Dad were always strapped for money, but they never talked finances in front of us. To this day, my brother and I do not know what Dad earned or what they had in their savings account.

Even as low as the rates were in those days, we always had a respect for the phone. We were allowed to make any call that we felt was necessary, but were always limited to the business at hand. Idle chatter, they said, was for school time or playtime. They followed the same rules. They talked the topic of the day and hung up. When Mom placed a call to her brother, Artie, and his wife Sheila in Detroit, she didn't always find both at home. She devised a signal system. She placed a person-to-person call for Sonya Pearl, the name of their infant daughter. The Detroiters would say that she would return in the number of minutes or hours when both of them would be there. Over the years, I have continued to fine tune the "signal" and have fun beating the system.

Dedication to family was our way of life. Whether right or wrong, the family always stood together, united to the world. If we had a disagreement, it was behind our own closed doors. Mom was a lady, but no one got away with a bad word about Dad. When Dad had his skin disease, Mom was always there for him. When Mom was sick, Dad was always there for her. Dr.Eli Stern, the family dentist said,[94] "Your parents were patients for a long time. Your mother was the quiet one. Your dad was very nurturing to her. He often came into the treatment room with her when she had treatment."

They always traveled together, socialized together, and loved life together. They were protective of each other and of their children.

A young girl, Beverly Halpern, lived in the house next to ours. She was on the heavy side, and I taunted her on this particular occasion. She retaliated by kicking me in the upper thigh. Mom took me over to her parents' apartment and, in front of her mother, told her to never do that again. If her kick was higher it "would have ruined him for life." Behind our own closed door, Mom told me not to taunt anyone again.

Our landlord at 9 Webster Avenue, Mr. Madoff would chase me whenever I played stoopball on the concrete steps. He would scream that the pink Spalding Ball was breaking the concrete and he would charge my parents for the repair. He was not a nice man. He would taunt me, yell at me, and chase me. I would run away and call him names. He wasn't crazy about the little athlete of seven years of age who lived on the second floor above him. Mom would always tell me to be careful not to damage people's property and not to worry about the rubber ball breaking the concrete.

One day, Mr. Madoff had been yelling at me for an extended period of time, and I couldn't take it anymore. I called him a rotten bastard. Well, he came after me, but I was saved by my Grandpa SAM, MOM'S DAD. Grandpa happened to be walking to my house when Mr. Madoff was chasing me. When Grandpa Sam asked the problem, Mr. Madoff only told him that I had cursed him. My clever grandpa diffused the situation by saying: "*Narasha mensh* (foolish man)! You listen to a seven-year-old boy."

Family. We were taught that was the most important thing in life. Honesty, integrity, and dedication to each other. What a legacy.

PUBLIC SCHOOL 192 was across the street from where I lived. After school, I lived in the schoolyard and played ball, that is, unless the college kids were playing ball, and then I had to watch. This particular day, I watched from the street outside the fence as one of the more powerful guys blasted a home run over the fence, across the street, and into a second floor window. I ran across the street to retrieve the ball and was immediately accused by the tenant of breaking her window. She came down, grabbed me by the shirt and took me to see my mother.

"Did you see him throw the ball through your window?" asked my Mom.

"No, but he was the only one there." accused the woman.

"My son says he did not do it, and I believe him."

I always told the truth, and my Mom always believed me.

There came a time when I wanted to go to the beach at Coney Island with my friends—without Mom. She would give me a lecture about undertow, tell me to be careful, hand me fifty cents and send me on my way. The cost of the excursion to the beach was forty-five cents. It was five cents for the Culver Line train in each direction. The summer train had bars for windows and an outside platform on each end of the car where we stood until we reached our destination; last stop, Coney Island. I always had two hot dogs and an orange drink at Nathan's, all for fifteen cents, then two rides at ten cents each. I always gave Mom the nickel change, unless we saved some of the fare. Either we would duck under the turnstile or two of us would go through at the same time and save the nickel in each direction. It was the thrill of saving the nickel that made us do it, because Mom was the beneficiary. I would give her a dime instead of a nickel.

Jewish Holidays Revisited

MOST OF THE JEWISH FESTIVALS are happy ones, but a few of the days of the year are solemn and serious. That is why they are called the High Holy Days. These are the days when our very lives are hanging in the balance before God. It is neither a happy nor a sad time. It is a time for deep thought. This extends over a period of ten days, also known as "the ten days of penitence." Incidentally, if the suit that I had been wearing no longer fit well, this was the time to buy a new one.

Only the first two days, Rosh Hashona, and the last one, Yom Kippur, are major festivals. They usually take place in mid-September to early October. The seven days in between are used by the Jews to improve our conduct so that in the *Book of Life*, God will write a favorable verdict for us. The special ceremony conducted on the first day of Rosh Hashona is called *Tashlich*, the casting of our sins. We go to a flowing body of water containing fish and shake out our clothing. Symbolically, we toss breadcrumbs into the water.

It is interesting to note that there are four names given to the New Year. Rosh Hashona is the most known and prevalently used name, and the only name not mentioned in the Torah.

God judges us for the upcoming year. That is why the holiday is known as *Yom Ha-Din*, The Day of Judgment. But in order to judge us fairly and justly, God remembers and weighs all our acts and deeds of the past year before He gives his final verdict. That is why it is also known as *Yom Ha-Zikaron*, The Day of Remembrance.

The fourth name of the holiday is *Yom T'ruah*, The Day of Sounding the *Shofar*, a ram's horn, which in ancient times was blown to announce an important event. That is why the Shofar is blown on this holiday. It is to remind the Jewish people to conduct themselves in an exemplary manner, holding themselves to a higher standard.

If someone says to you "*L'Shanah Tovah Teekatayvu*," they are saying: May you be inscribed in the *Book Of Life* for a Good Year.

YOM KIPPUR, THE DAY OF ATONEMENT, is the holiest day of the year. We ask for forgiveness of our sins. The *Book of Life*, on this sacred day, is closed and sealed until the next year. The special ceremony performed before the holiday begins is called *Shluggin Kapporos*. While repeating a prayer three times and swinging a fowl around our head once for each prayer, we offer the fowl's life as a substitute for us in asking for forgiveness. In the modern day, we substitute eighteen cents (eighteen means life, in Hebrew) for the fowl and then donate the money to charity. The Jewish day starts at sundown, so the holiday begins at sundown, at which time all Jews around the world start to fast—that is, they stop eating until well after sundown the following day.

It is on Yom Kippur that a Jew realizes why we feel bad when another Jew has sinned. Jews feel responsible for each other. When we ask for forgiveness, we mention sins that may have been committed by any Jew.

Mom would spend the day preparing the meal and cleaning the house before the fast. Dad would come home early and take a nap before the big meal. He would tell us that the men in his office would say the Jews were lucky because it never rained on Yom Kippur, except in 1946 when I was ten years old. (I remember that year because my brother threw up during the fast.) Dad's bosses and co-workers would taunt him about leaving early and make bad jokes about the Jews and their stupid holidays.

We would start the meal at about half past four in the evening so we could finish early and go to Shul for *Kol Nidre*, the opening hymn. That would be the official start of Yom Kippur. The meal started with a *borucha* (prayer) for a piece of *challah* that my father's mother made with white raisins. She made challahs with white raisins every Yom Kippur and several other times a year for me because she knew how much I loved white raisins. Every time I have challah with white raisins, I think of Grandma Annie. The significance of the honey was to symbolize a very sweet year. Then we said a prayer with the red wine, and the third prayer was said while eating a slice of skinned Macintosh apple with lots of honey. We would then have a salad followed by chicken soup and then flanken accompanied by two vegetables and potatoes. We would conclude the meal with applesauce or fruit cocktail.

After dinner, we turned off the lights in the house, and Mom would light a candle. No electricity would be used until the holiday was concluded the next night. Mom would take Marty and me to Shul, but Dad did not accompany us.

By 9:30 the next morning, Martin and I, dressed in our new suits, white shirts, and ties, would meet Grandpa Sam in his Shul on Twelfth Avenue and Forty-sixth Street. When it came to davening (praying), Grandpa was very strict. Every so often, when he saw our minds wandering, he would hit his *siddur*, the prayer book, with open palm and say "Daven." At the afternoon break, we would leave for home, wishing Grandpa a happy and healthy New Year.

In the early afternoon, the four of us would take a walk. This was a yearly ritual. After about a half hour, Dad would leave us, and Mom and her two sons would continue for another hour. I found out, years later, that Dad would go for a cup of coffee and a smoke. We would all arrive home at about four in the afternoon.

At half past five, Mom would take her boys to the Shul on Eighteenth Avenue and Fiftieth Street. The place was packed. The same stale odor was emanating every year. Mom would try to push me close to the front so I could see the man with the *tallit* (prayer shawl) over his head blow the Shofar, designating the end of the holiday.

The three of us would then rush home. Dad would have the salad made and the table set so we could start our "break-fast." It was always the same. We started with a prayer and challah with white raisins and lots of honey for a sweet year.

We next had melon with lots of honey for a sweet year. Mom only wanted sweet years for her men. She would always wish us a healthy, happy, sweet year.

L'Shana Tovah Teekataymu. May the Book be sealed giving you a good year.

FOLLOWING THE HIGH HOLIDAYS is the happiest of all festivals on the calendar. It is three festivals combined into one; *Sukkot, Sh'mini Atzeret,* and *Simhat Torah.*

Sukkot marked the end of the harvest when the Israelites brought their offerings to the temples as a sign of thanksgiving for God's kindness. During the forty years of wandering in the desert, after leaving Egypt, every Jewish family built a small, frail hut called a *sukkah* to protect them.

Mom showed me, whenever we went into a sukkah, that the slats of green branches were laid as a cover in such a way that there was more shade than light, yet also in such a way that you would still see the stars in the sky.

There were four species of growth that we still have today: the *etrog* which looks like a big lemon, and a *lulav*, which is a palm branch. Attached to the lulav were two other sets of leaves, willow and myrtle. I remember marching in the temple with the men and children, shaking the lulav.

Then we would eat and say *Kiddush* (prayer over the wine) in the sukkah.

THE LAST TWO DAYS of the Sukkot Festival are known as *Sh'mini Atzeret* and *Simchat Torah.* I didn't know that Sh'mini Atzeret was such a solemn day. Mom went to Shul on that day to say *Yizkor*, a prayer for the dead.

Simchat Torah marks the completion of the Torah readings. The Torah is rewound, and readings begin all over again. It is on this holiday that every Torah is removed from the ark and carried by a man around the temple, followed by children carrying flags with an apple stuck on the tip and sometimes a lighted candle inside the apple. Some children carry miniature Torahs. It was quite a sight, on this holiday, when I carried the Israeli Flag with an apple stuck in the top and a lit candle where the stem was removed. It was an impressive site to see all the other kids with the same flag, apple, and candle walking around the streets of Borough Park, following the men holding the Torahs.

The twenty-fifth of *Kislev* falls out in late November to late December. That is the start of the Jewish holiday of Chanukah, which lasts for eight days. The story is told of a madman Syrian king, Antiochus, who forced the Jews to live with the other people of the kingdom and worship the Greek gods. The Jews did not accept this and decided to rebel and fight the Syrians.

After the Jews, under the leadership of Judah Maccabee, beat the Syrians in the war, they cleaned out the old temple in Jerusalem of all the Greek gods.

When they went to light the Eternal Light, which stays lit all the time, they found enough oil for only one day. It took eight days to prepare the special oil. The Jews did not want to anger their God and prayed for a miracle. The oil lasted for the eight days until the new preparation became available, and this was the Miracle of Chanukah. To remind us of this wonderful miracle, we light one candle, plus the *shamos*, (servant candle used to light the other candles) every night for eight nights.

Dad would light the shamos, and each of the boys would light the remaining candles. The first night we would sing three prayers to usher in the holiday, and the remaining nights we would sing only one prayer. Then Mom and I would sing "*Maoz Tzur*," one of the Hebrew songs for this holiday.

This holiday encourages a form of gambling for children, using a popular top called a *dreidle*. There are four sides to the dreidle, and each side has a different Hebrew letter. Pennies are placed on the floor and one player spins the dreidle. If it falls on the letter *nun*, the player gets nothing. If it falls on the *gimmel*, the player gets all the money. If it lands on the *hay*, he gets half the pot, and if it lands on the *shin*, the player pays into the pot. Mom would play the dreidle game with me, starting me off with ten pennies. Somehow, I always won.

The house would always smell from potato *latkes* that Mom made several times during the holiday. We would add some applesauce to the pancake whose oil was absorbed on a brown paper bag, and they would be gobbled up quickly. I was the slowest eater in the family, but come Chanukah, I seemed to eat rather quickly.

I couldn't wait till dinner was done. That was when Martin and I received our Chanukah gifts and Chanukah *gelt* (money). Chanukah continues to be one of our happiest holidays. *Shehechiyonu, v'keyamonu, v'higionu, lazman hazeh*, gives thanks for the fact that He kept us in life, sustained and preserved us, and enabled us to reach this holiday.

More Stories from the Past

FRIENDS AND RELATIVES ALL spoke very highly of both Mom and Dad. My cousin Adrienne remembers Mom as a lady[95]. She said that, "when I was little, she spoke to me as though I was an adult. She told me about good manners, to keep my head erect and about being kind. She seemed gentle, kind, sweet and very loving."

I MET RICHARD COHEN when I entered college. We both joined the same fraternity, Sigma Phi Omega, and doubled-dated. The joke of the year was that I would get him a blind date one week, and his blind date would get me a blind date the next. We rotated getting each other blind dates because the girls didn't want to date us the second time.

I was the only one who called him Dick. When I called his house the first three times, his mother told me there was no Dick Cohen at that number, and hung up. Finally she said this is the Cohen residence and Dick and I were finally connected. I always got along very well with his parents, and we always joked about those three telephone calls. Mr. Cohen owned a hardware store. My father had a collection of tools, and I enjoyed talking to his father about new tools and old. We always had something to discuss. Back then, a young man always showed respect for his elders. That was something that was taught in the home.

DICK RECALLS[96] THAT "we go back a long way." He wrote:

> My contact and memories of your folks are indeed pleasant ones. Your dad was always very logical. He could explain things in great detail. He was a serious type but was very quick to laugh at a joke once you got him going. He was a great listener and a truly concerned friend and adviser. I remember him lending you the car for our double-dating days and his advice before we went out. He had a very high respect for your mom. I remember bumping into him on a few occasions in the Municipal Building on Chambers Street in Manhattan and receiving a smile and firm handshake. When we would meet, your dad was always interested in me and how I was doing. He must have been a great adviser, a dad who took a deep interest in his children.
>
> Your mom was always a lady; a polite, very sensible person who chatted briefly with me when I called. I even remember your phone number was In(dependence) 1-1121. She kept your apartment on Union Street very neat and organized. She, like your dad, was very organized and logical. I feel that they took a big interest in both you and Marty.
>
> Paul, it was a different world in those days; simpler but harder. Sugar was sugar, salt was salt, what you saw was usually what you got. No free lunches, except mom's sandwiches, which always tasted good. Your folks were educated, up on things and with the times.
>
> Thanks for the opportunity of going down memory lane with you. Your folks were a part of my life too. My memories of them were always of positive, pleasant, congenial, caring, and concerned parents. (See if she has a good-looking friend. Only kidding.) Your frat brother and long time friend."

MOM AND DAD PROVED that friendship is different from all other relationships. The lesson was passed on that friends never cheat each other, take advantage, or lie. They glory in each other's successes and are saddened by their failures. Friends minister to and nurse each other and stand always ready to help.

Dad was always giving of himself and helping others with no thought of remuneration. It was his greatest joy to help friends and family and observe the germination of the seeds of his knowledge. When I was stationed in Pensacola, Florida, as an officer on the staff of the Chief of Naval Air Training (CNATRA), the civilians working for me asked that I help survey a newly acquired property they had just purchased for the purpose of constructing a church. I spent several days surveying and preparing a contour map. They were shocked that a Jew would perform all that work for a Christian organization and not charge anything. As young as I was, I had learned my father's "giving way." They made a community luncheon in my honor as a thank-you for the work I had done.

My friends, Sandy and Elaine Cohen, remember Dad coming to their new store in Valley Stream and advising them on the most appropriate exterior door to use.[97] This door was used as the required second means of egress and led to a dark rear area of a number of stores.

Herman Stein, a friend of my brother's, remembers that Dad made up plans for his dental office "which functioned very well for over thirty years."[98]

When Ron Kolman, Mom and Dad's nephew, turned teenager, he was frustrated and aggravated with his inability to build a plan table.[99] While visiting his parents in Detroit, Dad helped him build the table and showed him how to use a T-square in conjunction with the table. Ron said, "Your dad showed me how to be precise without becoming aggravated."

Dad never hugged or kissed his boys. In that era, it was not considered the manly thing to do. He was proud of his sons and surely had good thoughts about them within. Outsiders observed how his face shone with pride when his boys did well, but the boys never received a pat on the back from him. He was quite different from Mom, who was swift with the compliments, both verbal and emotional. Mom was also the eternal optimist. "Things will always work out for the best," was one of her favorite sayings.

Dad was strict. He was the disciplinarian. When Mom thought that Dad was being too strict by not allowing us to pursue a harmless activity, she would use a Jewish expression that she thought I did not understand. She would say, *Luzem* (let him). Sometimes it worked, and Dad would relent—and sometimes he would be stubborn and stand his ground.

An organized basketball team, from coach to every player, wanted in the worst way for me to join. The prerequisite was membership in the YMHA—the Young Men's Hebrew Association—that required a $25 fee. Dad refused to pay. The team accompanied me back and forth between home to the Y, trying to convince the director to lower the fee for me and trying to convince my father to pay the now reduced nominal fee. Even when the director eliminated the fee completely, he refused. "If you are good enough to play organized ball, then get on your high school team," he said.

That was the year that New Utrecht High School won the city championship game against Flushing High School, and I *wasn't* good enough to make the team. Not being allowed to join the team from the Y was a crushing blow to my ego and an experience that I never forgot.

And yet, there were times when Dad was very patient with me. He taught me how to ride a two-wheeled bike. I remember him running along side the bike until I balanced myself, and that he came to pick me up when I fell. Then we started all over again.

I remember him teaching me to drive a car. My first lesson was to sit behind the wheel and, with the car in neutral, "press on the accelerator to get the feel of the gas pedal." Both Mom and Dad would tell me to drive with care. "Do not let anyone convince you to drive fast or in an unsafe manner." That lesson stayed with me forever. Be your own person and do not let anyone convince you to do anything that you think is immoral and unlawful.

It is interesting that so many people have said that Mom was a gracious lady, very warm and regal, and Dad was down-to-earth and warm with a great sense of humor. Lillie Reines, a friend of long-standing, said, "That is where Paul inherited his sense of humor."[100]

Dad's first cousin, Saul Sharison, who knew most of the Weinberg family, said that Dave was a wonderful, wonderful man. He was not only the most intellectual person in the whole family, he was very low key.

As much as many people talked about Dave Weinberg's helping hand, there were as many who talked about how Mom exuded warmth, sincerity, tenderness, and the ability to preserve privities. Rhoda (Pickholz) Reisner echoed what others said. "I just liked her. We got along so nicely together."[101] Rhoda discussed things and showed things to Mom that were very personal in nature that she would not discuss with any of her other friends or relatives. "I felt that whatever would be shown or discussed would remain a confidence, and it did."

Mom was a lady ahead of her time by many years. When she and Dad returned from their trip to Arizona, she brought back silver dollars that she said were going to be very valuable. She also brought back a necktie of a kind that was worn in the West. It looked like a heavy shoelace with silver ends and was tied together with a silver slide. That fashion came to the Eastern states several years later.

She took me to the United Nations shortly after the UN started to print stamps of its own. I still possess the envelopes stamped "First Day of Issue" of all the original United Nations stamps. Mom said that these stamps would be worth a lot of money some day.

Mom took Martin and me to many different shows, exhibits, landmarks, and sites of interest. Dell-O-Dell was called the "Queen of Magic" in the 1940s. Martin became a member of the "Friends of Magic" on April 14, 1944, and I became a member when I was Dell-O-Dell's assistant on February 5, 1945. She was known as the "World's Greatest Lady Magician." At about the same time, I was given a book called "Easy Tricks with Numbers," which contained 108 tricks for ages nine to ninety and opened the door into the magic world of numbers. The introduction to magic in different forms had such a profound affect on me that I started to write the math problems that Grandpa Sam gave me every time he saw me, and forty years later, I became an amateur magician.

Mom and Dad were always entertaining, whether it was friends or relatives, whether living nearby or visiting, and every visitor to the Weinberg's talked about their unique cup and saucer collection. Wherever they went, Mom purchased a single cup, saucer, cake plate, and a display piece of China. There came a time when her collection reached several dozen. When she served cake and coffee, it was always in one of her individually designed settings.

Mom found a place on MacDonald Avenue in Brooklyn that blended different flavored coffee beans from all over the world. The proprietor would keep a card file that listed the number of beans of each flavor that a customer ordered, so the customer could purchase the same blend, a variation blend, or a different blend altogether.

We ground the coffee fresh in our kitchen just prior to using it. In Brooklyn, we used a hand cranked coffee grinder, and our friends wanted the experience and privilege of grinding the coffee. When we moved to Flushing, we replaced the hand grinder with an electric grinder. Either way, guests liked to watch the beans being ground, and loved the aroma of the coffee as it wafted through the house.

Sam and Jeanne Berliner were Mom and Dad's friends. Jeanne[102] reminisced, "With your mother, you could eat off the floor. The most fastidious person I have ever met. Everything about her just shone. She had dishes that were all different and beautiful. Every time your mother took a trip she would buy something, and they were always tripping. Your mother was superb. I sinned on her fresh coffee and cake. She found a coffee grinder in an antique place, and it was mounted on the side of the kitchen cabinet. Every time they made coffee, it smelled out of this world. Your mother's specialty was good coffee. I don't know what chicken soup or pot roast she made, but her coffee was perfect."

On one of Mom and Dad's trips, they met Mildred and Irving Feingold. Mildred wrote, "My story begins at the St. Moritz Hotel in Miami Beach where we had the pleasure of meeting Dorothy and Dave. We became fast friends immediately. The men became shuffleboard champs." [103] Although the Finegolds lived in Montreal, Canada they continued their friendship by phone, visits, and cruises.

Mildred would say that "your mom and dad wanted so very much to see and know that their two sons were blessed with love and happiness," and continued, "there is no way to express the warmth your parents had for each other and their friends … and they will long be remembered."

My cousins Adrienne Sills and Barbara Regen always loved Mom's English bone china and how it was displayed. Barbara[104] tells a story of Mom back in 1967, the year after she married Stan.

> Stan and I had dinner at her house shortly after we were married. I was looking at her knickknacks while she briefly described the "when and where" of them. She took another one out of a cabinet to show me. I asked her why she didn't keep that one out for display, as it was just as beautiful and interesting as the others. She explained that because she had so many nice things and not nearly enough room to display them all at one time, she "rotated" them. Every few months, she would put some away and display others. That way, she got to see all the lovely things she had accumulated through her travels over the years…. As I accumulated my own beautiful pieces, I adopted the practice of "rotating" every six months. My things seem new to me and, at the same time, bring back wonderful memories. My kids knew why I did this, and they loved helping to wrap and unwrap all my things. Perhaps they, too, will use your Mom's good idea.

Whoever came to the Weinberg's apartment always left raving about the beaded curtains in the kitchen and bath that Mom handcrafted. The beaded curtains were complemented by beaded flowers and, soon after, chenille flowers. She shared her knowledge and her creations with anyone who wanted to learn the craft or have the flowers adorn their own home. When Mom's cousin, Yahuda Gur-Arie and his family came from Israel to the United States for a temporary stay, Mom and Dad entertained them. Their young children, Ann, ten, and Gilat, nine, were "turned on" by the hobby and remember how Mom taught them how to do it. "We really enjoyed it. It was a nice pastime."[105]

The adjectives used for Mom and Dad were many.

For Mom: the penultimate lady, ahead of her time, exuded warmth and sincerity, nurturing, good ear for listening, graceful and regal, great cook and housekeeper, confidence builder, keeps a secret, kind, poised, quick with praise, and a warmly loved and loveable person.

For Dad: the penultimate gentleman, kind and giving, knowledgeable, logical, neat and well organized, productive, keeper of the "gum drawer," a good sense of humor, very mechanically inclined, problem solver extraordinaire, a strict disciplinarian, and well-liked.

They both possessed attributes described by the adjectives: personally active in charities, creative, dedicated friend, diplomatic, energetic, always ready to help others, great advisor, sharing, and talented.

It would be very difficult to find two people who possessed so many fine traits as Dave and Dorothy Weinberg did.

Samson Schussler (circa 1955)

Dave and Dorothy Weinberg, Flushing, N.Y. Apartment
First Seder night, Passover (Apr 4,1966)
Dave, Dottie, Paul, Linda, Martin, Elaine,
on laps: Elyce, Stacy, Mona, Sheryl

7

Dorothy's Last Years

IN THIS CHAPTER, which commences in 1954, the year I turned eighteen, I will refer to Dottie and Dave by either their given names or as Mom and Dad. Because of the personal, vivid memories of my relationship with them, when I'm involved in the vignette, I'll refer to them as Mom and Dad.

IN THE EYES OF SOME RELIGIOUS Jews, when a new home is purchased, good things happen. Dave and Dottie were living in their new apartment in Flushing, and by 1954, Dave's skin condition had become much more tolerable. It continued to improve, just as the family doctor had predicted. "It will go, just the way it came. No one will know the cause of its coming, and no one will know how or why it cleared. It will just, one day, disappear." And it did.

Although the next twenty-two years had some unhappy events, those years encompassed the happiest times of their lives. They move to an upscale cooperative apartment. Dave becomes a vice president in a bank that has always securely surrounded itself with the proverbial White Anglo Saxon Protestant leadership. Their younger son follows in the lead of their older son by graduating from a prestigious engineering college and becoming an officer in the United States Navy. They see lots of *naches* (gratification from their children) as their two sons marry and produce offspring who adore their grandparents. Vacations of cruises and trips become a usual event.

Mom was in all her glory. She loved the new apartment and the new surroundings. She was the perfect neighbor. While Dave was working, Dottie was spreading the pollen of goodwill among their neighbors. There was no one who did not like Dottie. Even the teenagers admired her. She organized the Franconia Teen Society by posting messages on the respective bulletin boards of each building and advising all teens to come to the first meeting at her apartment. Paul became good friends with Les Krasnagor, who went on to become a pulmonary doctor. There must have been twenty young people, ranging in age from thirteen to nineteen, partaking of Dottie's refreshments and listening to her ideas. She organized the first teen dance in the Franconia C Building Recreation Room.

DOTTIE LOVED TO DANCE and wanted her boys to follow in her footsteps. She was so graceful. When she went on a dance floor, especially on special occasions such as weddings or bar mitzvahs, people would admire her grace as she floated across the room. Dancing with her son Paul was a highlight for her. She organized a dance club consisting of several married young couples in the co-op and had a dance instructor come to her apartment once a week to give lessons. Phil and Florence Smith, the neighbors from the other end of the second floor, would always be the first ones to arrive for the lesson. Although Phil was a bit on the heavy side, he danced well and followed the beat. Dave, still with his two left feet, tried to do the cha-cha, but he readily admitted that he didn't hear the beat of the drum, and was very happy to be led around the floor by his graceful wife.

But Dottie passed on her dancing grace to Paul. Paul's older buddy, Herb Schlossberg, a brilliant electrical engineer and partner in one of the largest mechanical consulting firms in the city, lived a few floors above and would often visit, solve engineering problems with Paul and then dance with Dottie to show off the new steps the young single people were doing in the clubs.

Yet, with all the activities that she had during the course of the day, at the end of the day, Mom always had dinner ready for the family. It was always a different balanced meal every night and something that we all enjoyed. Dad would break out in hives when he ate strawberries or mushrooms, but Martin liked mushrooms, and I liked strawberries, so there were times when different meals were served on the same night so everyone enjoyed the dinner.

When Mom and Dad purchased their apartment, it became very quickly known that Dave was in the construction industry and extremely knowledgeable in both construction and real estate laws. He was quickly nominated and voted to the Franconia board of directors and spent an inordinate amount of time inspecting the property to verify compliance with plans, specifications and the law. Many of his evenings were spent with other directors determining the course of action they should take with both the builder and the management agent, or the financial position of the corporation, or who should be hired to long—and short-term positions, who should do the interviewing, what equipment should or should not be purchased, etc. Although this pro bono work was a time-consuming burden, it was personally challenging and rewarding, not in a monetary way, but because he gained respect from his peers.

DOTTIE WAS CULTIVATING her artistic and decorating abilities. She developed two new hobbies; one was making flowers from specially dyed and treated paper, and another was the creation of flowers and window decorations with the use of extremely tiny but colorful beads. She was always very talented with her hands, making sweaters, bootie moccasins (I still have the sweater and booties she made for me), as well as blankets, sweaters, booties, and more for her granddaughters. Her beaded flowers are still exhibited, to this day, in our home. The flowers are of multiple colors, and if you stand five feet from the bouquet, you can only see a beautiful floral arrangement and no individual bead. Kitchen and bath windows were adorned with beaded curtains. Her sister Annette still keeps her bath window draped with the beaded curtains. Many people said that Dottie had a flare for decorating, dressing, and designing that were well ahead of her time.

MOM ALSO NEVER FORGOT her obligation to teach her sons the "lessons of life." When I was growing up, there was a great cultural shift toward children and teenagers. They were no longer treated as little men. Mom indulged my needs for play and fun and encouraged good friendships. The Cub Scouts and Boy Scouts were healthy places of learning. She never had to send our friends away because we listened when she said, "Remember birds of a feather flock together, or you're judged by the company you keep." She taught and reinforced the edict that "Character Counts." She knew that it was not easy to defy peer pressure and educational standards that were starting to diminish. But she wanted her boys to be responsible for their deeds, have an understanding that one is measured by concepts of respect, honor, civility, integrity, humility and personal accountability. She made it clear that she expected us to be responsible not only for what we did, but also for what we failed to do. She was always the lady, Dad always the gentleman, and she wanted her boys to grow up to be gentlemen too.

I REMEMBER THAT MOM AND DAD had a good sense of humor. Dad was the joke teller and Mom was the *kibitzer*. They also had a sense of family that always came first. Mom bragged about the family, but was always humble. She always considered me the baby. When I objected to her use of that term, she lovingly told me that I "would always be 'her baby' until the day she died." From that time till her death, I embraced that term.

After graduating from the Polytechnic Institute of Technology with a degree in civil engineering, Martin went into the United States Navy and began tolerating his time as the public works officer at Camp Lejune, North Carolina.

Paul was a student in a pre-engineering course in Brooklyn College. When the family moved from Brooklyn to Flushing during his first year, he transferred into the engineering curriculum at the City College of New York. He became active in the teen movement that Dottie had started and also became the coach of the Little League pre-teenagers. The kids loved Paul. He would use Dave's car and make several round trips to drive them to Kissena Park for practice and for games. Although none of the parents helped with either the driving or coaching, many were critical of the amount of playing time given to their kids. In June of 1955, Paul broke his wrist jumping over a fence for a ball. He couldn't drive that summer, and still the fathers would not help, but the team admired their coach for continuing their baseball training through the entire summer.

Before graduating college, he became a hero of the co-op. A six-year-old boy who was living with his parents on the sixth floor of the C building found his way out of the apartment without anyone knowing and took the stairs to the roof. I heard a commotion in the street below my second floor apartment, looked out, and saw all eyes turned up. They told me that Josh was standing on the parapet wall on the roof. I had babysat for the boy, and I loved him as he loved me. I bolted out the apartment door and took the stairs two steps at a time and quietly eased open the roof door. There was Josh, one step away from oblivion. Not wanting to frighten him, I called to him and he turned to look me in the eye, as if to say, "What am I doing here? Help me." I calmly talked as I slowly approached him with my arms outstretched. He put his arms out and hugged me when I got to the wall and took him down.

ON SEPTEMBER 24, 1955, even though Martin was in the navy and Paul was just recuperating from his broken wrist, the two made a twenty-fifth wedding anniversary party for their parents in the recreation room of Franconia Village. It was the first party that the boys had made for their parents, they had fun doing it, and all the guests had an enjoyable time. One of the guests was Larry Goldberg, a cantor, and he performed the remarriage ceremony in front of all the friends and relatives.

DAVE'S MOTHER'S HEALTH began to decline. A heavy smoker, Dave was going through two packs of cigarettes a day. But when his mother went into a coma in early 1959, he increased to three packs a day. Between the stress of his mother's condition and the three packs of cigarettes, he lost his voice. The doctor suggested that he reduce the number of cigarettes back to two packs and see what happens. But as his mother's condition worsened, so did his voice.

On the evening of April 14, 1959, Paul watched the following event unfold.

Dad and I were standing in the foyer, when Dad took from his shirt pocket a pack containing just six cigarettes. He snapped his middle finger at the bottom of the pack and out shot one cigarette, which he placed between his nicotine, stained lips. As he replaced the pack in his pocket, he took out his cigarette lighter, and with his right thumb, snapped on the flame. As he brought the light to the cigarette, he paused, released the pressure of his thumb and said, "What am I doing?" The lighter went back into his pocket, he retrieved the pack of five cigarettes, and returned the cigarette to the pack. He never smoked again.[106]

It is my opinion that Dad stopped smoking for more than one reason. The main reason was that it was adversely affecting his health. The second reason was his feeling that the secondhand smoke was adversely affecting Mom.

The smokers in the bank were merciless. When they noticed Dave not smoking, they taunted him by blowing smoke in his face and reminding him how smoking was so wonderful and relaxing. They couldn't believe that Dave would have the self-control to resist the temptation of a smoke when they offered him cigarettes. But Dave had developed his own method of self-control. He kept the pack of six cigarettes and the lighter in his upper left shirt pocket for the next two months, challenging himself to restrain from the ugly habit. It worked.

That was a tough year. The Ma, Annie Weinberg, Dave's mother, died on May 28, 1959. She never got to hear how her son became an officer of a bank. She would have been proud.

The health of the Pa was also deteriorating, and he became almost totally blind. He couldn't bear living without the Ma.

MY MOTHER, DOTTIE, developed an asthmatic condition that would get much worse for several years before it improved. Speculation was that the cause was allergic reaction to foods, stress from Dave's illness, and reaction to some of the dyes and oils in the paper goods she was using to make artificial flowers. The condition did grow worse. They researched and found the best allergy doctor in the field, a Dr. Murray Peshkin, president of the Children's Asthmatic Foundation that was raising money to build a hospital in Denver. Dottie and Dave became very involved with Dr. Peshkin's foundation, and, over a period of years, were so instrumental in raising large sums of money for the project that they received many awards for their dedicated work.

There were times that Dottie found it difficult to breathe. They brought oxygen tanks to the apartment and kept them at her bedside. Every night she would have to use it to help her breathe. The doctor put her through a series of scratch tests to determine the allergies, but to no avail. The situation worsened, and Dottie was hospitalized. The doctor put her through a new aggressive program developed by Dr. Peshkin, and placed her on an all liquid diet for a week. She was in a very weakened state and her condition was very serious. At that point, the doctor added different solid foods to her diet to determine which, if any, was the cause of the trouble. Slowly, she regained her strength and was allowed to return home.

It is interesting to note how stress causes tangential health problems.

As a matter of interest, there were two things that Mom and Dad never shared with Martin and me. The first was the amount of money Dad was earning. They felt that we should not share in any of the family's financial pressure. The second was any pain and anguish they suffered by virtue of their own illnesses or those of their friends and family. We were to be free of that emotional burden.

THE YEAR 1961 was one of the happiest years in Mom's life. She was deeply involved in the planning of two weddings. Martin was married to Elaine on June 25, 1961. Paul was in the navy at that time, and all the arrangements for *his* wedding to Linda were being made, exclusively, by Dottie and Linda. Dave and Dottie paid for half of all the expenses of both weddings and all the expenses of the *aufruf*.

The aufruf is a tradition practiced for centuries to initiate the round of wedding celebrations, in which the groom is called to the Torah before the wedding. Its purpose, also, is to publicly announce the forthcoming nuptials. After the reading of the Torah and the groom's concluding blessing, the congregation supplements the mazel tovs by throwing nuts and raisins at the groom.[107] Sometimes a party is held where all the friends and relatives have the first official opportunity to congratulate the groom and meet the beautiful bride. Mom and Dad made the party in the recreation room in Franconia Village. It was a frelach event.

Linda and Paul's wedding, which took place on July 30, 1961, was perfect. Everything from the color coordinated gold *yarmulkes* and the gold dresses of the bridesmaids, to the food, the band, the flowers, and the specialty items, were all done in perfect taste.

But the Pa was very weak and blind and was unable to attend either of the weddings.

Meanwhile, in addition to all the work he was doing for the bank, Dave continued to do private work for Arthur J. Quinn, who had been hired in 1943 and had, in the early 1960s become the new president of the merged banks, now called the New York Bank for Savings. Dave also worked privately for Mr. Quinn's family. Everyone at the bank knew that whatever Dave designed would get swift approval in the City Building Department. His peers and his immediate bosses never got over the resentment that they felt at *the Jew* being able to get things approved so fast. The relationship of the president and Dave had grown warm, and on February 5, 1962, Dave received a promotion to vice president of the bank, with a title of executive assistant.

After the promotion, he was assigned a new executive secretary who said:

> He was a special person. He was a gentleman. He was *always* a gentleman. Never got angry. If he did, you never knew it. He was even tempered all the time. He had a lot of friends in and out of the bank and always treated me with the utmost respect. I remember when he spoke to your mom, how nice he spoke to her. I always thought what a nice man he was and what a wonderful husband he must be. He used to tell me how ill she was with the asthma, and how difficult it was for her to sleep. He was very patient and spoke of her very lovingly.
>
> Dolsen Rauscher was his immediate boss. They got along well. I don't think they were friends. Everybody was stuffy. He always called him Mr. Rauscher. I don't think he ever called him Dolsen. I think he got along as well as boss and worker can get along. Mr. Rauscher was tough. We just did as we were told. Everybody was like that. But your dad was a very smart man. He did a lot for the bank. When things had to get done with approvals, he got it done. Not that he did anything illegal; he just got it done quicker.[108]

Another corporate officer said that Dave was a "hard worker and one who knew his business."[109]

Dave's father, whose health was failing, heard about his favorite son's promotion. Although a very proud father, he never told him how proud he was of his achievements. The Pa, Nathan Weinberg, died on April 18, 1962. It was on the first Seder night of Passover.

DOTTIE KNEW THAT DAVE was a bundle of nerves, was all stressed out, and had to have a rest. She, too, had to have a break and a change of scenery, and so she arranged for their first real vacation. They spent the next few weeks in Jamaica and Puerto Rico. It was the start of the most relaxed time of their married life. Idolized by friends and family for their loving ways and happy for Dave's well-deserved promotion, everyone was glad to see them get away for a while.

SINCE LINDA WAS PREGNANT with their first child, Paul obtained early release from the navy. They took a five-week auto trip starting in Pensacola, Florida, where they were living. After vacationing in Miami Beach for a week, they leisurely traveled up the East Coast and across to Detroit, Michigan to visit Dottie's brother Artie and family. The final stop before going home was Niagara Falls. Mom knew the day and the time of Linda and Paul's arrival and made a welcome home surprise party for them. Typical Mom; "make parties."

Now it was Dottie's father, Samson Aaron, whose health failed. He died on October 3, 1962.

After apartment hunting for several months, Linda and Paul settled into a small two-bedroom apartment across the street from Dottie and Dave. Dottie was thrilled. She saw her granddaughters—Stacy Ann, who was named after Dottie's father, and a year later another granddaughter, Elyce—any time she wanted by just crossing the street and visiting. Mom was not an intruder. She would always call and ask if she could visit and then take the girls on day trips; this relieved Linda from her everyday chores and gave Grandma Dottie the opportunity to enjoy "her girls." The girls grew very attached to Grandma Dottie.

AT THE END OF THE YEAR, one in which Dave and Dottie both lost their fathers, they took their first cruise, which was on the Greek Line TSS *Olympia*, visiting the ports of St. Thomas, Puerto Rico, Trinidad, Caracas in Venezuela, and Curacao. Dottie loved the trip. "Look at all I have been missing." She then decided there would be many more trips in the future.

Meanwhile, the president of the bank, recognizing Dave's continual propensity for excellence in work ethic and output, gave him another promotion. On August 20, 1963, just eighteen months after his promotion to executive assistant, Dave received his next raise and promotion to *principal* executive assistant.

The harder Dave worked, the more plans Dottie made for the next vacation. It was on May 22, 1966, that the two of them embarked on an American Jewish Congress thirty-day trip to Israel and three countries in Europe, flying El Al Airlines from John F. Kennedy International Airport in New York. Dottie had always wanted to live long enough to see the state of Israel. They spent the first fifteen days touring all of Israel. Dottie loved the Jewish history and, while there, even found time to find some relatives. They visited her cousin, Yahuda, his wife, Elsa and their two children Ann and Gilat. Israel was the highlight of the trip. Leaving, they went on to visit Rome and Florence, Lucerne and Paris, and then to London before returning home on June 30.

Travel was in Dottie's blood. On January 2, 1967, they cruised the Bahamas for eighteen days. In September of that year, they traveled to Detroit, Michigan, and to Toronto and Montreal, Canada, to visit relatives and friends.

Whether Dave felt he owed something to the bank for continuing his salary while he was ill, or it was just part of him to give an honest day's work for a day's pay, or perhaps a combination of both, he worked hard and produced well for the bank. Dottie felt that his dedication should be rewarded, and on November 4, 1968, they took their next big trip. They went to Japan, Taiwan, Singapore, Thailand, Bangkok, Hong Kong, Victoria, The Walled City, Aberdeen, and Honolulu.

Dottie was in all her glory. The good health wish was always on her tongue. She longed to travel with Dave, cater to all his needs, dance together, hug and kiss. Everything she wanted was there.

The day before Paul's thirty-third birthday, November 8, 1969, they took off for a tour of the West Coast and visited San Francisco, Los Angeles, Palm Springs, Las Vegas, Grand Canyon, and Yosemite national parks, dipping into Mexico to see Nogales, then to Tucson before returning home. It was a prelude to Dave's impending retirement the following year.

THE YEAR 1970 was a year of celebrations. Dottie had always told her boys to, "Make parties. You never know when your time or someone else's time will come, so make parties for all happy events." Her sons received the message early in life, and this year was the time for Martin and Paul to make a gala for their parents, so they sent formal invitations to seventy-eight people.

The party took place in Martin and Elaine's backyard. Paul had a dance floor built and hired an accordion player to play both dance music and background music for the afternoon. All of Dottie and Dave's aunts, cousins, brothers and sisters, and their children were invited, along with all their friends. The men wore jackets and ties, and all the women were dressed in their finest. Dottie always enjoyed being with her grandchildren, Mona, Stacy, Elyce, and Sheryl, and she received the biggest gift of all when "her four girls" sang and danced for her.

Dottie's cousin, Seymour, who had introduced Dottie and Dave more than forty years earlier, was there to wish them mazel tov. Everyone in attendance was a very special part of Dave and Dottie's life. Two of those not attending were Uncle Max and Aunt Olga who were living in Berlin, but they did send a telegram saying that their thoughts were there in wishing them a happy anniversary.

A large double layer cake was ordered. The top layer, which was as thick as the bottom layer, was adorned with the numbers 4 and 0 and the words, "Happy Anniversary Mother and Dad." The drinks flowed, and the food was consumed all afternoon, culminating in the singing of "Happy Anniversary to Dottie and Dave." The happy couple seemed to have a smile glued to their faces all day.

The letter they sent to their children and spouses read:

> Since we came home from the party, we have been searching for the proper
> words, but we find that there are no adequate words to express our gratitude
> towards both of you for the fortieth wedding anniversary party you made for
> us. Although we have blessed you over and over again for the joys you have
> extended us, I thought we could do better by spelling it out. But no matter
> how we tried, there just are no suitable words to be found.
>
> "Thank You" comes from deep down in the bottom of our hearts. It can-
> not go deeper. No matter how many times we will say it or write it, at the
> present time our only wish is that your children will always give you the
> respect and joy you have given us. And may you both have joys and content-
> ment with good health and love for each other always.
>
> Our kindest and best wishes and love are always for you.

IN THE BUSINESS WORLD at the New York Bank for Savings, President Arthur J.
Quinn's last chance to say, "Thank you, Dave, for the great job you have done
for the bank," came on January 1, 1970. On that day, Dave was given his final
promotion to assistant secretary, the title he held until his retirement on October
21, 1970.

It is my opinion that Dave, in addition to being well respected by his peers,
was now also well liked. One of the parties made by his peers was held by Dolsen
Rauscher at an afternoon outdoor cookout at his home on the shores of Culver
Lake in New Jersey.

Dave had come a long way since October 14, 1935, when he was hired for one
month as a temporary architectural draftsman. He worked himself up to a high,
honorable position in a prestigious bank in New York City, overcoming the bur-
dens and hurdles of major hatred for the token Jew.

It was now time to think about the retirement years, and Dottie and Dave
thought about living in Florida for four or five of the winter months and the rest
of the year living near their children and grandchildren, who at this time were living in their own homes on Long Island. Before selling their cooperative apartment in Flushing, they tried out this new adventure for two years, found it very
pleasing, and then took the "deep plunge" by selling the co-op and most of their
furniture and moving south. It was quite traumatic, because they were moving
away from their children; that was a difficult idea to digest, especially for Dottie.
They rented a one-bedroom apartment at 7525 E. Treasure Drive in North Bay
Village in North Miami Beach, referred to as "Treasure Island." The apartment
was on the sixth floor of a high-rise apartment building, right next to a two-mile-
long boardwalk abutting a very picturesque waterway. They would live here for

the next six years, having their children and grandchildren come visit them every winter. The pool in front of the apartment house allowed Grandma and Grandpa to watch their kiddies swim and show off.

The apartment was decorated with bright new furniture for the living room, painted white with pretty green foliage. It included a pullout sofa bed that slept two. A new bedroom set with a brass and cut glass backboard was just what she wanted to match the new chest of drawers. Although the kitchen was small, the dining room was certainly large enough to accommodate a group of their friends for dinner or an end of evening "coffee and cake."

Linda and Paul looked forward to their company during the summer. Paul took his father with him to his jobs and got some interesting feedback. Linda thoroughly enjoyed being with her mother-in-law. I don't know who adored who more. And, of course, Grandma Dottie had her chance to "eat up" her grandchildren. There was a beautiful chemistry between them. It was also a time when Paul and his father solidified their relationship. Dave was always anxious to build or repair something in the house, and Paul loved his father's help.

IT WAS IN 1974 that things began to unravel. Dottie developed back pains that eventually could not be treated at home. They were living in Florida, and Dave had a hard time with the doctors' responses to his questions. After talking with Dad one night, I called Martin and we agreed to book the next flight out of New York to help Dad with some emotional decisions. I had developed a good relationship with Dad, so my job would be to calm him. Martin, who was technical, was to ask all the questions of the doctors. When I told Dad that we were on the way down, I heard an audible sigh of relief.

Before surgery on her spine, Mom told me that if they discovered cancer in her body, it would be her wish to die. "I do not want to live like a vegetable." Two days later, she underwent surgery. Martin went home. I stayed. As my mother had done for me when I was born, I did for her now. I was at her bedside all day, and I fed her her first solid meal that night. She never remembered my doing it, but I will never forget the good feeling I had helping my mom.

I decided to stay in the hospital until the crisis passed, despite the nurses asking me to leave. I'm glad I did. At about 11 PM, I noticed that she was breathing heavily, and the graph was showing a flattening trend. Since there were no beepers, buzzers, or bells at the nurses' station, she could have died right then. I ran out and got the nurse to look in on Mom. When she recognized the emergency situation, she immediately gave her a shot of something and got her breathing back to normal. I spent a few more hours in the hospital, making sure things were stabilized, before going back to my parents' apartment alone, with the good feeling that I just saved my mom's life.

Dad had developed a kidney stone the day of Mom's surgery and underwent his own surgery at the same hospital the next day. His room was one floor above Mom, so I visited him when he was awake and alert and spent the rest of the time holding onto my mother's hand and watching all the equipment that was attached to her. When Dad was released from the hospital, Mom was awake and alert, and I felt much better about going home.

MOM SPENT A LONG TIME in the hospital and a rehabilitation center, learning how to stand and walk without the use of a cane. It was a rough time for her, but Dad was there with her all the time, waiting on her every whim, just like she had done for him when he was infected with his skin disease.

It was a year of rehabilitation. She worked very hard and painfully to bring herself back to what she had been before the surgery, and she was quite successful. After about three months, the cane was put into storage, never to be used again. Now began the work on strengthening her legs and back. Her constitution was strong, and she was determined. It paid off. By the summer of 1975, Mom had made it back, and as they did every summer, Mom and Dad took leave of Florida to be with their children and grandchildren.

Before leaving to return to Florida, they made sure to attend the bat mitzvah of their oldest grandchild, Mona, on October 5, 1975. On January 23, 1976, they made a return trip to attend Stacy's bat mitzvah. Mom looked radiant in her floral print dress. She was so beautiful and graceful on the dance floor, giving no indication of any pain. However, this was to be her last formal family affair.

They returned to Florida, but Mom's health seemed to be taking a downturn. She wasn't feeling up to her exuberant self. She went to many different doctors, taking many different tests that all came up negative. However, there was fear in their hearts that something serious was brewing. As was their usual practice, they came to New York in April 1976.

As I write this chapter, I realize that diagnostic medicine in 1976 was nowhere as good as it is today, and I am sure it will continue to get better.

Dad wrote a letter to his friends and relatives around the country and Canada that his boys did not see until after his death. The letter read:

Dear Folks:

You must forgive us for not writing to you any sooner, but so many things have happened to us lately that we did not know whether we were coming or going. Let me explain:

During the early part of June, Dottie suddenly came down with severe pains, swelling of the veins and ugly redness in the left arm, that then traveled to the left calf, then traveled to the right calf and to the right thigh, and when it landed in the crotch the doctor ordered immediate hospitalization. He called it severe migratory phlebitis and was concerned that it may hit the lungs or the heart. On June 11, she was admitted as an emergency case, and they started work on her immediately and fortunately were able to catch it and control it, but after it had subsided, the doctors had to find out what caused such a sudden and widespread flare up. They had to find out so that they could treat the illness properly, and, should it happen again, they wanted to know what they could do to treat it again.

Well, in the course of investigations, tests, x-rays, scans, etc, etc, Dottie was so mutilated, hurt, morally depressed, etc., that she had no will to go on. The doctors, at the same time, did not help us morally either, because they indicated the worst. Yes, I mean the worst, and for over a week we dreaded hearing any reports of the tests. Finally, last week, the doctors said that most of the tests, etc., were negative, and then we started to breathe again. In a couple of days, she will be taking the barium enema and GI series to try to rule out other things or to find the cause. After we received the report that the tests were negative, Dottie developed pains in the chest. After tests and sophisticated x-rays, they discovered that a clot had broken away and landed on her chest. Another scare and further treatment finally cleared up most of this clot. Now we feel and hope that she is on the road to recovery, but we still do not know how long she will be in the hospital. The hospital is located in the Bronx, the Albert Einstein Hospital, which is one of the best, and I am staying in Merrick with my son (Paul), and traveling from here to the Bronx is very tiring, grueling and going through what we did, weakened me to such an extent that I too became sick, and this is the first opportunity that I have had to write to you.

Other than the above, all is well with us, hope all is well with you too. Let's hear from you.

Love and regards

P.S. Please forgive typing and copies of this letter.

Linda and I owned two cars and had given my father one for his daily travel to be with Mom. Linda would get up early and drive me to the station with our two girls so I could take the train to work in the city. It was a sacrifice that had to be made in order to allow Dad to see Mom every day.

Mom always said that things work out for the best and everything will be all right. One of her Jewish expressions was things are *beshert*; things are destined.

On July 1, 1976, Dad gave Mom "A Birthday Love Note." The printed portion was a poem that read:

It seems there's little time in our busy, hectic life
For telling you I love you and I'm proud that you're my wife
And though this loving little note is for your birthday, Dear
My thoughts, my wishes, and my love are yours all through the year!

Dad wrote the following:

> To my Darling Wife Dottie:
>   Although you are in the Hospital now, you will be cured and we will both be *Happy* and *Healthy* together. With all my love.
> Your loving husband,
> Dave

Although she was in pain and uncomfortable, she was released from the hospital and returned to my house where she lay on the couch in the living room with her legs elevated, in accordance with the doctors instructions, to ease the pain and keep the swelling in her legs to a minimum. I never heard my mother complain. She would read, get up and do some activities with Dad, perhaps take a small walk or take a ride somewhere, but always go back to the couch as the sun went down.

Mom wanted, in the worst way, to make a fifteenth anniversary party for her boys and their spouses. Sheryl remembers that she and Mona made one for her parents. "In my eyes she (Grandma Dottie) was fine. Whatever pain and discomfort she was in, it never showed to me. She was always there with a smiling, happy face."[110]

But the pains intensified and she didn't have the strength to make any more party arrangements. Stacy and Elyce did not have the fun of making a surprise party with Grandma for their Mom and Dad.

The pain became unbearable towards the end of July, and she went back to the hospital, never to return. She had a nurse whose maiden name was Weinberg, and my father became friendly with her. She was kind. She was the one who told us that the type of cancer my mother had would take her life in three months to a year. It would create much pain in the patient, so the family had better bond together. It would not be an easy time for anyone.

I could not bring myself to believe that my mother would die at such an early age. I would go to work every day and visit my mother three times during the week and Saturday and Sunday, still not believing that I would be losing her within the year.

On October 16, 1976, Mom's condition took a turn for the worse. She slipped in and out of a coma. There was no way anyone could communicate with her. At this time, I was coming to the hospital every night after work. It was very stressful knowing that Mom was losing the war against the cancer that had invaded and spread throughout her body.

I put my head on her pillow, and the tears of a forty-year-old man were streaming down as I tenderly held her hand and stroked her thin black and blue arm and told her I loved her and wished she could hear me and wished she could tell me, once again, that she loved me.

Many years earlier, I had seen a movie in which a murderer was on trial. He had taken one person's life and destroyed the life of another. In the courtroom scene, the poor woman, whose life was now relegated to a wheel chair by the defendant's dastardly act, couldn't speak. Her body was paralyzed. Her son would hold her hand and get his mother to respond to his questions by the squeeze of her hand. And so, by her responses to yes and no questions, squeezing with her hand once or twice, the murderer was convicted.

I put my mouth close to Mom's ear and whispered, "I love you. If you hear me, squeeze my hand once." My heart felt like it leapt out of my shirt when she squeezed my hand. "If you love me, squeeze my hand once." Another squeeze. "Squeeze once for yes and twice for no. Do you know everyone in the room?" Squeeze, squeeze. She did not know.

And so, knowing the time we had to speak to each other was limited, I lay there and talked with Mom until they asked me to leave the hospital.

The next night, October 17, Mom was very bad. The nurse said she had no more feelings and would probably die that night. She scratched the bottom of Mom's feet and said if there was any life left in her, there would be a reaction to the scratch on this most tender part of the body.

When the nurse left, Mom and I talked again until, once again, they asked me to leave the hospital. I would whisper loving thoughts into her ear and she would squeeze my hand in response. The squeezes were very weak, but we told each other, "I love you." I always kissed Mom before leaving.

October 18 was the last visit. Mom was not even responding to the squeeze. Dad, Linda, and I left the hospital at 8:30 PM after telling her that she was loved. Dad kissed her, knowing …

Since the day in May when Mom entered the hospital, except for those many nights he had spent with her there, he had slept alone on the pullout sofa bed in the den. After a long day at the hospital during which he would never leave her side, Dad would come back to my house and fall exhausted into bed, just as he did this evening.

The call came at 10:30 that night. Dad was sleeping. I asked the doctor to stay on the phone while I woke my father. I kneeled at the edge of the bed and whispered, "Dad," to wake him. When he woke, I said "It's Mom." From the light in the foyer, I saw his glazed eyes as he said, "She's gone?"

Elaine and Martin Wedding (June 25, 1961)

Martin graduation from
Officer Candidate School (July 8, 1953)

Paul and Linda Wedding (July 30, 1961)

Paul graduation from
Officer Candidate School (Nov 18, 1959)

Weinberg children and grandchildren
At their Flushing apartment, (June 1, 1973)
Back: Martin, Elaine, Linda, Paul
Front: Mona, Sheryl, Elyce, Stacy

Dave and Dottie, (January 1976)

8

David's Last Years

IN THIS CHAPTER, I will refer to myself as I rather than as Paul.

MOM DID NOT DIE. "Things always work out for the best. It's beshert." Tomorrow I'll visit Mom and we'll have a nice chat about my fortieth birthday party next month. We will also talk about the bat mitzvah that is being planned for Elyce in January. "You know you like 'to make parties.'" That's what we'll talk about; parties and celebrations. "You will look so graceful on the dance floor. Right, Mom? Mom, are you there? Mom, I don't hear you. Where did you go, Mom?"

I called Martin after the doctor told me that Mom had died. He and Elaine came to my house after midnight, and we called the rabbi. The girls were asleep, so the five of us talked about what each one of us would do and the arrangements that would have to be made for the funeral, hiring a funeral parlor, selecting a coffin, etc., and making a list as to who would be notified. I was in a daze. I didn't believe what had happened, but I had to put on a calm face.

We woke Stacy and hugged her as she cried bitterly. Stacy loved her Grandma Dottie. They had a very special relationship, and she would feel the pain of the loss for a long time.

It was a most difficult time for Dave and his boys. I, for one, was in a daze for the next several weeks. I remember, on October 20, two days after she died, walking with our family down Path forty-one in the Mount Zion Cemetery in Maspeth, New York to grave number 163, not believing what would now happen. I was turning the shovel the wrong way and tossing dirt onto a coffin containing my best friend. *"Yisgadal v'yiskadash sh'me rabbo"* is what I was saying. No, no, this can't be. This is really a bad dream. As we walked back to the car, my cousin, Adrienne, held my arm and tried very hard to comfort me.

Every morning for the following seven days, Dad, Martin and I went to Temple Israel in South Merrick to say the prayers for Mom. As I write this part of the story, I realize it was a very traumatic part of my life. It was a time when I did not believe in the reality of the events of the past three months, the reality of the three final days of Mom's life in the hospital, and the finality of the internment. In a way it was good that I had to return to work after a week; it brought me back to real life. The next seventeen years, for Dad, however, were marked with a conglomeration of happiness, sadness, and frustration.

Cantor Bauer was at Martin's house every night conducting services for the family and the friends who came to pay a Shiva call. On November 1, I wrote a letter to the cantor that said:

> Dear Cantor Bauer,
>   It is two weeks since the passing of our mother and wife. The clouds of sadness still hang heavy upon us but slowly we are able to see the brightness beyond and remember the beauty of the things she left behind.
>   We also remember the spiritual help you gave us during the period of Shiva. On behalf of David, Martin and his family, and Paul and his family we want you to accept the enclosed check as a token of our appreciation.

I signed it: The Weinberg Family.

WHEN MOM DIED, I didn't want to believe it. She always said, "Things happen for the best," so I felt that tomorrow she would be there talking to me, listening to me, being my best friend. Isn't it interesting that I just took her for granted while she was there for me, as old as I was, and yet when she was gone, there was that awful void in my life.

Dad stayed with Linda and me for the next several months before returning to his apartment in Florida. I regret that I did not accompany him, but he insisted that he travel alone. He felt it was important for him to stabilize himself, and that the best way to achieve that goal was to do it alone. I still feel that I should have accompanied him. However, Sid and Millie Kalikow did insist that they go with him, and they did fly down to Miami and stayed with him for a few days. I never forgot the kindness they bestowed on my father in his time of grief.

When Mom and Dad first moved to Florida, I felt they would live a more relaxing life in the warm sunny south. My happiness was diminished by sadness. Sad because I would not be able to see them as much as I would if they were living in New York, within a forty minute drive, and sad that my children would not have Grandma Dottie and Grandpa Dave full time.

After Mom died and Dad returned to the apartment in Florida, I felt cheated. I did not feel that Dad cheated me. After all, he had all his friends living in south

Florida, and his two brothers and two sisters were living within a short drive. However, I felt that I would not have the opportunity to confide in my father long-distance the way I could if he were living here, and the way I did when we visited.

To give him a choice of location, Linda and I offered to build an extension to our house and have him stay with us in the privacy of his own room. There was no hesitation in his response. He had become comfortable living in Florida, and the move back to New York would isolate him from his contemporaries. I also felt that he did not want to be a burden. One other reason was that Dad and I had developed the best rapport of our lives, and he may not have wanted it tarnished in any way by our living under one roof.

Dad had that uncanny, unique knack of looking at things from many different angles. Martin and I would have been there for him, no matter what his request. However, he had so many more family members and friends that made his support team quite vast.

Dad did have invitations to be with other people, and he accepted those invitations. In reciprocation, he took his friends out for dinner because he couldn't make dinner by himself at home. Basically though, Dad stayed by himself for the next twelve months, mourning the death of his wife, Dottie. His friends offered to introduce him to single women who were widowed or divorced, but he always refused. This was a year of mourning.

We would speak to each other at least once a week, and he seemed to be adjusting to life on his own. Linda and I would visit him several times a year, but we could tell he was no longer complete. He never purchased anything for himself. When we went down to visit, we would help him pick out and purchase clothes and other accessories he needed. Linda taught him how to make flanken, one of his favorite dishes, and other meat and vegetable dishes for dinner. Living alone was taking a toll.

He put on a good act of being satisfied with life, knowing that he couldn't do anything about what had happened to his wife. I am sure there were tears some nights. Dad would tell me that the things he missed most were the conversations, the companionship, the caring, and the kiss good night. He missed lying in bed at night and talking and feeling someone next to him. Part of him died when Mom died.

At this stage of his life, he needed someone to care for him, to keep him company, and someone who would need and appreciate what he had to offer to make him more complete. He was a good man who could provide companionship, do the male chores around the house, who would drive wherever necessary, manage the money and do the taxes, the shopping, the packing of clothes for trips, the arrangements for flights and taxi rides, and all the fixing of broken or damaged items.

After mourning for an entire year, Dad's friends introduced him to female companions, something Martin and I could not have easily done. Dad started to accept offers to meet eligible women, and on one of our visits, we met one of those ladies. Dad knew what he wanted and what he did not want. He did not want a woman with lots of money who would feel that she could make all the decisions based on her wealth. He wanted a woman who was a lady. He wanted a woman who would take care of his needs and someone he could care for.

IT WAS THE FALL OF 1977, two months shy of the first anniversary of Mom's death that Martin and Elaine moved to Florida. The home building business in Nassau and Suffolk Counties of New York was drying up, and Martin decided that the market in south Florida provided a better opportunity. Martin was flying down for weeks at a time to survey the market, meet other contractors and sub-contractors, learn the requirements of the various municipal agencies, make application for a professional engineering license and a contractor's license so that he would be ready to get a jump-start on a business the moment the family moved. Elaine accompanied him on several trips, and they purchased a ranch style home in Hollywood.

The timing was perfect, not only for Martin and family, but for Dad. Dad would now have his oldest son a twenty-minute ride and a local phone call away. The older generation did not like to make long-distance phone calls because of the high cost. When Mom and Dad moved to Florida, we had communicated by sending audiotapes to each other. Of course the cost for long-distance calls had come way down from the time they first got their telephone on Webster Avenue in 1936, but the habit of making short local calls and even shorter long-distance calls was very ingrained.

Time passed. It was now more than two years since Mom died, and Dad was actively looking for a companion. In February 1979, he told me that he had met a woman by the name of *Miriam Deutsch,* and that they were contemplating marriage. He asked if we would like to meet her. Linda and I booked a flight to Florida and met with them. She was a charming woman who kept an immaculate apartment in Hallandale and had a gift for writing.

Linda and I arrived in time to celebrate Miriam's sixty-ninth birthday on March 1, and Dad's seventy-third birthday on March 17. They would always celebrate their birthdays at the same time. When we returned home, we received a letter in which she wrote, "Needless to say, it was my pleasure to meet your dad's beautiful family. You are all warm, outgoing, and most generous. You made me feel comfortable, relaxed, and part of you." She continued by saying, "I'm confident when you all meet, the offspring from our respective families will have a favorable rapport with one another too. In closing, please accept my deep thanks for everything. I love my plant and birthday remembrance."[111]

On May 30, the lease on the apartment that Dad was renting would expire. He either had to renew it for a year or vacate the premises. So now there was pressure on him to either obligate himself for another year or get married and move into Miriam's apartment. The decision had to be made now. Should he get married and move out, or wait another year? He decided to marry before the end of April so that he would have the month of May to move all his belongings without any pressure.

Dad was a very bright man, but he always listened to the opinions of others. Now that the decision was made, what precautions should he take regarding the protection of his estate—including all the possessions accumulated with Mom that he wanted to go to his sons and each of their children? He was cognizant of the problems created when a new spouse, who was introduced into a new family died. To whom would the estate go? Dad insisted that they have a pre-nuptial agreement drawn and signed. Although one attorney drew the agreement, each party had the opportunity to consult separately with independent legal counsel regarding his or her legal rights.

On April 23 they both signed the nine-page agreement detailing the rights and obligations of each party.

Four days later they were married.

April 27, 1979, was a warm, sunny day in Florida. Martin and I held two posts of the chuppah and two of Mim's sons held the other two. The wedding ceremony was short, and we all celebrated by having dinner together.

Miriam, known to all as *Mim*, had four sons. The newlyweds expressed the hope that the boys would be friends and socialize. After the wedding, the six sons and their wives waved them off to cruise the Caribbean for their honeymoon, and then all went their separate ways. Dad always felt that relationships were built on mutual respect. He was intelligent, kept up a conversation, and played life's give-and-take game to the fullest. He was always there to help a friend or relative and expected the same treatment in return. He was independent and proud to the point of being aggressive if he felt someone was taking advantage of him. Yet he knew, through life's experiences, when he had to back off and when he had to divest himself of authority and responsibility. And so he conducted himself as a gentleman throughout the life of this second marriage.

Although Dad had inherited a new family, it was his own family that provided him warmth and love. He would continue to be embraced by those who loved and admired him. Sheryl, his youngest granddaughter, observed that "Grandpa's life ended when Grandma's life ended. Marrying Mim, yes, he moved on. I don't think his life was to the fullest. He had a more enjoyable life with Grandma Dottie. They shared more and experienced more. He was doing more for others than himself. That was good for Grandpa. He lived through us."[112]

His eldest granddaughter, Mona, said that her "relationship with Grandpa improved after Grandma passed away because it was only him that I was focusing on." After Grandma died "Grandpa wanted to be involved with everything. He was anxious to hear everything that was going on in my life, especially after we moved to Florida. He wanted us to visit and come with the kids. He wanted to know how everybody was doing. When he was sick, he would still want to know about everybody else. When my kids were sick and he was very, very sick, he would call about my kids."[113]

Linda and I continued to speak to Dad at least once a week and visit him annually with Stacy and Elyce. He and Mim would come to New York and stay with us every year. Dad and I would visit every job in which my construction company was involved, and he gave excellent suggestions and constructive ideas. He loved it, and I felt he would have been more involved if he lived in New York.

In October of 1992, Martin called me to tell me that Dad had been diagnosed with cancer of the bladder. Linda and I went to Florida and, together with Martin and Elaine, discussed the situation with his oncologist, Dr. Herbert Brizel, who said that the tumor could be treated with radiation to decrease the size and increase the chances of lengthening his life. If left unchecked, he would probably die within three months.

Despite having radiation, things were deteriorating with Dad and his cancer. It started to grow again and to metastasize. I found myself traveling to and from Florida to see him quite frequently and could not attend to my business. At the end of 1992, I closed the doors to my business and kept in touch with Dad on a more frequent basis. By March 1993, his eighty-seventh birthday, we placed him in a nursing home and he was shuttled to and from the hospital whenever the need arose. One of those times was to place a feeding tube into his stomach. As things were going from bad to worse, Dad was shuttled from one location to the next. He was hospitalized at the Hollywood Memorial Hospital and shortly sent to the Palm Gardens Nursing Home. When it was evident that the situation would not improve, Martin and I decided that the right thing to do, to keep him comfortable, was to have him moved to a hospice.

On June 3, 1993, he went to the Hollywood Medical Center Hospice where the very caring staff kept him comfortable. Linda and I arrived in Florida a few days later. Martin, Elaine, and Linda and I remained at his bedside the better part of every day. I did with Dad what I had done with Mom seventeen years earlier. He was so weak that he couldn't speak, so I spoke to him by squeezing hands. On June 7 and June 8 he was responsive to my squeezing communication. On June 9 his response ceased.

At 9:30 in the morning on June 10, we received a call from the hospice that he was fading fast and was going to die soon. We rushed to the hospice, but it was too late. Dad had died. It was only after researching information for this book that I uncovered the fact that his death came sixty-four years to the very day after he and my mother first walked together on the boardwalk at Coney Island.

Although I was involved in the contract with the funeral home prior to Dad's death, it was Martin who had done the major portion of the work. When Dad died, someone from the mortuary staff came to the hospice and took the body to the funeral home in Florida for services over which Rabbi Konigsberg presided.

After the services, the funeral home provided for the body to be flown to New York for internment next to Mom. It was not easy for me, even at the age of fifty-seven, to realize that my parents were gone. Dad's death affected me both emotionally and physically for more than a year.

Rabbi Maurice Simckes led the memorial service at the Gutterman's Funeral Parlor in Rockville Center. This is what he said in his eulogy:[114]

> David and his wife Dorothy (Dottie) had a most beautiful, wonderful marriage founded upon the pillars of mutual love, respect, faith, trust and devotion. Through good times and through difficult times they walked hand in hand through the path of life for forty-six blessed years. They were truly a mutually devoted couple until she passed away seventeen years ago.
>
> Paul and Martin, you remember a devoted, self-sacrificing and understanding father who was always there for you. He worked hard all of his life to provide for you, but was never too busy to discuss the important things in your lives as you were growing up. He was always there to guide you, to teach you, to provide you with the background so that you would become respected members of your respective communities. You especially remember the encouragement and the optimism that he instilled in you, the drive to be a success at whatever you do, and above all, the ethics that he imparted to you.

David Weinberg had a loving, caring, and mutual respectful relationship with his daughters-in-law, Linda and Elaine. David was especially devoted and dedicated to his family. He loved to be with them, to spend time with them.

He was a very special grandfather to his beloved grandchildren and great grandchildren, Stacy and her husband Steve and their daughter Darci, Elyce and her husband Mitch, and their daughter Molly, Mona and her husband Steve, and their children Ashley and Corey, Sheryl and her husband Mark, and their children Matthew and Danielle. They were the apples of his eye, and he was so very happy when he was with them. Symbolic of the sentiments of the entire family was the fact that his oldest great grandchild, Matthew, looked up to heaven the day after his passing and said, "Grandpa, I love you."

David had a great relationship with his brother Irving, his brother Mac, who is deceased, his sisters Gladys and Frances, as well as with their spouses and his nieces and nephews.

David had a good marriage for fourteen years with Miriam. He got along well with her family as well. It is a shame that she too is ill at this time.

David loved working with his hands in carpentry, electrical work, plumbing, and he even dabbled in watch making. If it was mechanical, chances are he could repair it. He had *"goldeneh hent."* His expertise in architecture and design was legendary and extraordinary. He was an expert in filing plans with the building department, and they respected his abilities. He loved to paint pictures, especially of landscapes. In his youth, he loved to play handball.

David Weinberg was a giving, good-natured human being. He never forgot a birthday, anniversary, Chanukah or special occasion. He was always anxious to help others—his sons, family, friends and neighbors. He loved to help build and repair things around the house. He was on the board of his condominium in Florida as well. His advice was respected there as it was in the co-op in Queens where he served in a similar capacity. He was also an honored member of the Kissena Jewish Center in Queens and Temple Sinai in Florida.

David Weinberg was a very industrious human being. He was an upstanding man of integrity who lived the words that he spoke. He was the type of man about whom an unkind word was rarely, if ever, spoken, for there was nothing unkind that could be said about this fine, honest gentleman. His principles of business were extraordinary. He was a vice president of the New York Bank for Savings in the Real Estate Department, a bank in which he served admirably for over thirty-five years. He was respected and admired by all of his colleagues and by the clients he served.

His credo was, MY WORD IS MY BOND.

Paul, Dave, Martin (1976)

Paul, Dave, Annette, Etta,
Mary (sitting), Linda (January 1993)

Endnotes

1. Zeichenerklarung, General Maps of Middle Europe

2. Seymour, Charlie and Sylvia Schussler, interview by author, tape recording, January 14, 1998.

3. Ship of Travel, *Patricia*, passenger record.

4. Sam Schussler and Perl Kummel's certificate of marriage.

5. Dora Schussler's certificate of birth.

6. *Encyclopedia Judaica* (New York: Collier-Macmillan, 1971), Vol. 13 p.27.

7. Miriam Weiner, *Jewish Roots in Poland* (Secaucus, NJ: Miriam Weiner Routes to Roots Foundation, 1997), p.9.

8. *The Universal Jewish Encyclopedia* Vol. 8 p.346.

9. Irving Howe, *World of our Fathers* (New York: Harcourt Brace Jovanovich, 1976), p.6.

10. *Encyclopedia Judaica* Vol. 14 p.444

11. Ibid.

12. World Book Encyclopedia, 2006, Vol. 16 s.v. "Nicholas ll" p.551.

13. *The New Encyclopedia Britannica* 15th ed. 2007, Vol. 7 s.v. "Lu-Shun" p.531.

14. Ibid, Vol. 26 s.v. "Russia Foreign Policy" p.991.

15. Arthur Kligler, interview by author, tape recording, February 15, 1998.

16. *Encyclopedia Americana International Edition*, 2006 Vol 24 s.v. "Russo-Japanese War" p.47.

17. R. Ernest Dupuy and Trevor Nevitt Dupuy, The *Harper Encyclopedia of Military History,* 4th ed. (New York, NY: HarperCollins, 1993), p.1008.

18. Howe, p.21.

19. *Yiddish Lodz: A Yizkor Book* (Melborn, Oystraliye: Lodzsher Tsenter in Melborn, 1974)

20. Lillie Kates quote from a Marsha Mayzel e-mail message to author, March 19, 1998.

21. *The Bible*, Leviticus 19:29

22. *Encyclopedia Judaica* Vol.14 p.563.

23. Lillie Kates, interview by author, tape recording, February 22, 1998.

24. Saul Sharison, interview by author, tape recording, February 6, 1998.

25. 1910 Federal Census of the United States of America

26. Nathan Weinberg's U.S. certificate of naturalization.

27. 1920 Federal Census of the United States of America

28. David Weinberg application for social security account number, Nov 24, 1936

29. 1915 State of New York Census

30. 1910 Federal Census of the United States of America

31. Certificate of Birth (delayed registration) for David Weinberg, June 6, 1962

32. A.A. Hoehling, The Great Epidemic (Boston, Little, Brown, 1961), prologue

33. *World Almanac and Book of Facts*, 2008

34. Mildred Kalikow (Dorothy's sister), interview by author, tape recording, August 11, 1997.

35. Artie (Oscar) Schussler (Dorothy's brother), interview by author, tape recording, November 17, 1997.

36. Charlie Schussler (Dorothy's cousin), interview by author, tape recording, January 14, 1998.

37. Mildred Kalikow, interview.

38. Howe, p.262.

39. Seymour Schussler (Dorothy's cousin), interview.

40. Seymour Schussler, conversations with author, 1998–1999

41. Etta Salant (Dorothy's sister), interview by author, tape recording, August 11, 1997.

42. P.S. 168 graduation exercises pamphlet, 1920.

43. Gladys Goldblatt, interview by author, tape recording, November 22, 1997.

44. Commercial High School, Brooklyn, N.Y., Arista certificate, October 23, 1923.

45. *Senior Ledger of Commercial High School,* Brooklyn, NY, June 1924.

46. Discussions with my dad throughout our lives.

47. U.S. Bureau of the Census, 1910.

48. U.S. Bureau of the Census, 1920.

49. Calendar pad of December 29, 1929.

50. Mildred Kalikow, interview.

51. Rabbi Elyohu Blasz, *The Code of Jewish Family Purity,* 13th ed. (Monsey, N.Y.: Committee for the Preservation of Jewish Family Purity, 1991).

52. *The Bible,* Leviticus 20:7

53. The *New York Times,* September 6, 1930

54. Zohar 1,91, b.

55. Wedding photographs of David and Dorothy Weinberg.

56. Marriage certificate of David and Dorothy Weinberg.

57. Maurice Lamm, *The Jewish Way In Love and Marriage.*

58. Rabbi Aryeh Kaplan, *Made in Heaven, A Jewish Wedding Guide* (New York: Moznaim Pub. Corp., 1983). 160 and Nathan Ausubel, *The Book of Jewish Knowledge,* p.491.

59. Elizabeth Burchenal, *Folk-Dances and Singing Games,* (New York: G. Schirmer, 1938)

60. Martin Weinberg, Certificate and Record of Birth

61. *Encyclopedia Judaica* Vol 11 p.1026.

62. *The Bible,* Genesis 2:18,24.

63. *New York Times,* June 20, 1931

64. Mildred Kalikow, interview

65. *Columbia University College of Physicians & Surgeons Complete Home Medical Guide*, rev 3d ed. (New York: Crown Publishers, 1995) and T*he Merck Manual of Medical Information*, Home ed. (Whitehouse Station, N.J.: MerckResearch Laboratories, 1997)

66. Martin Weinberg, interview by author, tape recording, January 13, 1998.

67. John (Jack) Westney, interview by author, tape recording, July 29, 1997.

68. George and Irene Burch, interview by author, tape recording, July 28, 1997.

69. Arthur Spier, *The Comprehensive Hebrew Calendar* 1900–2000 (New York: Behrman House, 1952)

70. Paul Weinberg's Circumcision certificate and book.

71. David Weinberg application for social security account number, November 24, 1936

72. *Vital Statistics of the United States*

73. *The World Book Encyclopedia,* (2006), Vol. P s.v. "Pneumonia" p.586.

74. R. Edgar Hope-Simpson, *The Transmission of Epidemic Influenza* (New York: Plenum Press, 1992), p.77.

75. Jeanne Berliner, interview by author, tape recording, January 13, 1998.

76. Jerome Pickholz, e-mail to author, March 1, 1999.

77. Nathan Ausubel, The Book of Jewish Knowledge, 1964

78. Pauline Block, letter to author

79. Morris Golomb, *Know Your Festivals and Enjoy Them* (New York: Shengold Publishers, 1973)

80. Linda Weinberg, written memories, January 19, 1999.

81. Myrna Barg, letter to author, July 1, 1997.

82. Elaine Weinberg, interview by author, January 13, 1998.

83. Mona (Weinberg) Miller, interview by author, August 5, 1999.

84. Stacy (Weinberg) Miller, interview by author, March 5, 1999.

85. Elyce (Weinberg) Neuhauser, written memories, December 15, 1998.

86. Sheryl (Weinberg) Scheer, interview by author, July 5, 1999.

87. Martin Weinberg, interview.

88. Millie Kalikow, e-mail dated November 20, 1998.

89. Arthur (Oscar) Schussler, e-mail, dated November 27, 1999.

90. Etta Salant, letter to author, received June 18, 1997.

91. Annette Schussler, letter to author, received June 17, 1997.

92. Charles Schussler, letter to author, July 6,1997.

93. Jerome Pickholz, letter to author, received September 4, 1997.

94. Dr. Eli Stern, letter to author, received July 23, 1997.

95. Adrienne Sills, letter to author, received June 15, 1997.

96. Dick Cohen, letter to author, received September 27, 1997

97. Elaine and Sandy Cohen, e-mail to author, June 18, 1997.

98. Herman Stein, letter to author, June 16, 1997.

99. Ron (Schussler) Kolman, interview by author, August 3, 1997.

100. Lillie Reines, e-mail to author, August 25, 1997.

101. Rhoda (Pickholz) Reisner, interview by author, July 18, 1997.

102. Jeanne Berliner, interview by author, tape recording, January 13, 1998.

103. Mildred Feingold, letters to author, 1997–1999.

104. Barbara Regen, e-mail to author, June 26, 1997.

105. Ann (Gur-Arie) Kelman, interview by author, tape recording, June 8, 1998.

106. David Weinberg's personal calendar of events.

107. Lamm, *The Jewish Way In Love And Marriage*

108. Estelle Garcia, interview by author, tape recording, June 1, 1998.

109. JJ Fischer, letter to author, August 25, 1997.

110. Sheryl (Weinberg) Scheer, interview

111. Miriam Deutsch letter, March 7, 1979

112. Sheryl Scheer, interview

113. Mona Miller, interview

114. Rabbi Maurice Simckes, eulogy, June 13, 1993 at Gutterman's Funeral Home, Rockville Centre, N.Y.

Epilogue

IT IS NINETY-FIVE YEARS after the birth of David Weinberg that we find two of his great grandchildren, Jacob David Neuhauser and Nolan David Miller, both of whom have been named after him, playing in the home of their grandfather, Paul, one of David's sons. Both Jacob and Nolan are six years of age and have two older sisters. Darci Loryn Miller, who just turned ten, and is the first child in the family to be named after her great grandmother, Dorothy (Schussler) Weinberg is playing with her first cousin, Molly Rose Neuhauser.

The girls are playing with their numerous American Girl Dolls, some of which are dressed in clothing from Dorothy's era. The cousins are very pretty, loving, and bright and bring a memory of the great grandmother after whom Darci is named.

The boys are playing with toy cars, trucks, Legos, and anything else they can bang around. They also enjoy playing with a handheld computer game called Game Boy that makes them think, and think quickly.

Their Grandpa Paul always challenges the four children with math related problems and puzzles just the way Dorothy's father had challenged him. It is a tradition that is handed down to the next generation.

Dorothy was always very artistic and made beautiful things with her hands. It has been said by many of her friends and relatives that she came before her generation. Grandpa Paul passes on to the next generation his artistic craft of origami, as well as his exciting hobby of magic.

Yes, the children will be the ones who link generation to generation and not allow the names of David and Dorothy to fade from memory.

978-0-595-44625-4
0-595-44625-6

www.ingramcontent.com/pod-product-compliance
Lightning Source LLC
Chambersburg PA
CBHW020430290526
45785CB00002B/783

* 9 7 8 0 5 9 5 4 4 6 2 5 4 *